One-way or Round Trip

Women Flight Attendants and Troops During the Vietnam War

John Culea

To KEVIN —
THANKS FOR YOUR FRIENDSHIP
AND BEING ON THE PRISON BEAT WITH ME.
THANKS FOR YOUR LOVE FOR THE
LORD, YOUR FAMILY & OUR
COUNTRY.

6-2-19

Cover Photo Courtesy:
The Pan Am Historical Foundation

Also by John Culea

Novels:
Light the Night
Best Moves
In the Air * On the Air
Air Apparent

Historical Fiction:
The Trail through Mohawk
The Rails through Mohawk
The Highway through Mohawk
Target Tombstone
Miner Leaguer
SanDiegoLand
Expo 2 Padres 1
Infamy to Injustice: Liberty's Shame

Non-Fiction:
The Hub Shootout
Takes, Outtakes & Bloopers

May 2019
John Culea
9019 Stargaze Avenue
San Diego, CA 92129
john.culea@gmail.com
(858) 484-5118

To Patti and all your fellow flight attendants who served courageously during the Vietnam War.

CONTENTS

Introduction

Between 1966 and 1975 more than a thousand flight attendants helped airlift many of the 2.7 million American men and women who served in the Vietnam War. Nearly all of the flight attendants were women.

For the troops who survived the war, theirs would be a round-trip flight but for more than 58,000 others and 2,500 prisoners of war or missing in action and 1,200 Americans reported killed in action but no body recovered, it was a one-way journey.

My wife, Patti Medaris (Culea) was one of those flight attendants. While her story and those of other flight attendants are featured in the book, their experiences mirrored all who walked the aisles serving men and women who went to battle. It is time that she and those who pinned on their wings receive the recognition they so richly deserve.

Chapter 1
Pretty Little Lights

In the early morning hours before sunrise in October 1967, a Flying Tiger Line Boeing 707 was on approach to the airport in Da Nang, South Vietnam. The plane with a crew of ten was one of 20 civilian airlines contracted to take thousands of American military troops in an out of the combat zone.

Over Da Nang 1967

But on this trip, the jetliner had no passengers. As soon as the plane landed it would be refueled and readied for a flight out of Da Nang loaded with troops who had completed their tour of duty. They were going home.

One of the flight attendants on board the Flying Tiger 707 that morning, making her first flight was newly hired 25-year-old Patti Medaris, a stunning, dark-haired beauty not quite five feet tall who was up front with the pilots for a view of the ground below.

Patti was born 34 years too early to fulfill a lifelong dream of being a combat jet fighter pilot, so she seized the opportunity to do the next best thing and became a flight attendant, first with Bonanza Airlines in Phoenix in 1962 before joining Flying Tiger Line in 1967.

Patti Medaris   Bonanza F-27
Bonanza Airlines 1962

On that October 1967 morning with Da Nang in sight, she was strapped in behind the pilot and co-pilot and while listening to ground control telling the pilots what runway to use and giving weather conditions, she leaned forward and peered out the cockpit window.

In the distance she saw a tremendous burst of sparkling, colorful lights.

With a lilt in her voice she asked, "Ooooh, what are all those pretty little lights?"

The pilot matter-of-factly responded, "They're shooting at us."

* * * * *

Patti remembers her first instinct was to lift her feet off the floor and then sheepishly realized that would hardly protect her from bullets that were following the tracers.

Whenever flak was in the air, pilots knew they had to get the plane on the ground as soon as possible, which the captain did and just after touchdown he opened the lift dumper panels on the wings to act as air brakes. Once the nose wheel was on the ground he engaged the engine's reverse thrust and used the main wheel brakes while quickly heading to an exit taxiway.

Da Nang 1967

Fifty-one years later, Patti remembered the feeling of relief in the cockpit that morning but little conversation other than the normal interchange between the pilot, co-pilot, flight engineer, navigator and air traffic controllers.

Once the plane came to a stop, Patti unbuckled herself and joined five other flight attendants in opening the aircraft for more than 200 troops who were now walking to the plane from the terminal. The 707 would be on the ground for less than an hour for refueling and then back in the air with the crew and a fully loaded plane of soldiers and Marines hoping to avoid anti-aircraft flak.

* * * * *

Vietnam has been fought over for thousands of years and may be the most militaristic of all countries in Southeast Asia. The shooting started when Vietnam began using firearms from the Ming dynasty in the late 14th century.

Five hundred years later on April 25, 1882, French Captain Henri Riviere illegally captured Hanoi. Although the city was returned to the Vietnamese,

Emperor Tu Duc was forced to accept French rule over central and northern Vietnam.

On September 22, 1940, Japan invaded French Indochina in a battle that lasted just four days. Japan wanted to stop China from importing arms and fuel from the port of Haiphong through Hanoi to the Chinese city of Kunming.

The Japanese were allowed to occupy Tonkin and that effectively blockaded China but when Japan surrendered to the U.S. following the bombing of Hiroshima and Nagasaki, the region was divided into four countries: North Vietnam, South Vietnam, Laos and what became known as Cambodia.

After World War II in 1946, France claimed Vietnam as a colony.

French Marine commandos land on Annam coast 1950

But French control ended on May 7, 1954. Following a four-month siege, rebels led by Ho Chi Mihn overran the French-held garrison at Dien Bien Phu.

Ho Chi Minh and Marius Moutet 1946

All of Ho's supporters went north and all French supporters headed south. Elections were supposed to reunite the country, but the United States opposed them fearing Ho would win the presidency. The U.S. backed Ngo Dinh Diem, a corrupt authoritarian and within a few years, Ho led a rebellion against Diem that included assassinations of non-Communist village leaders.

Economic and military aid to fight Communist rebels came from presidents Truman, Eisenhower, Kennedy and Johnson. America also sent military advisors with some taking part in raids despite claims they were there only to help the South's self-defense.

The U.S. trained and directed South Vietnamese commandos to blow up radar stations, bridges and other targets along the North Vietnamese coast. American warships conducted electronic espionage missions to get intelligence for South Vietnam.

A major turning point came on November 2, 1963 when President Diem was murdered in a CIA-backed coup d'état.

Ngo Dinh Diem

Eight months later, events in Vietnam began happening that would change America forever.

On July 31, 1964, U.S.-backed patrol boats shelled two North Vietnamese islands in the Gulf of Tonkin. The destroyer USS Maddox headed to the area.

USS Maddox

On August 2, as Maddox cruised along the coast, three Soviet-built, North Vietnamese torpedo boats challenged the destroyer to chase it away.

U.S. Navy photo of three torpedo boats approaching USS Maddox

The Maddox fired warning shots but the three boats continued their approach and opened up with machine-gun and torpedo fire.

Four F-8 Crusader jets were scrambled from the nearby aircraft carrier Ticonderoga and were soon over the scene.

F-8E Crusader

The jets, using Zuni rockets and the Maddox firing its 5-inch guns, badly damaged at least one of the North Vietnamese boats. One of the Crusader jets took machine gun fire and despite having a large portion of its wing shot off, made it back safely to the Ticonderoga.

Only one bullet from the attacking boats found its mark on the Maddox and harmlessly lodged in its superstructure.

The next day, the U.S. destroyer Turner Joy was sent to reinforce the Maddox as U.S.-backed raids were made against two more North Vietnamese defense positions.

USS Turner Joy

Then on August 4, the Maddox and Turner Joy reported being ambushed by enemy boats; claiming 22 torpedoes had been fired at them.

In response, President Lyndon Johnson ordered air strikes against North Vietnamese boat bases and an oil storage depot.

Lyndon Johnson

That night, LBJ addressed the nation in a televised speech saying, "Aggression by terror against the peaceful villagers of South Vietnam has now been joined by open aggression on the high seas against the United States of America." He also asked for a congressional resolution, known as the Gulf of Tonkin Resolution. It was passed unanimously in the House and opposed by only two senators, Democrats Wayne Morse of Oregon and Ernest Gruening of Alaska. The president had the power to wage war in

Southeast Asia anyway he wanted.

Years later the true story of what happened in the Gulf of Tonkin proved
the destroyers were not on routine patrol in international waters; they were
on an espionage mission in waters claimed by North Vietnam. The Johnson
administration said the two attacks were unprovoked but never disclosed the
U.S.-backed raids that were going on at the same time. But an even bigger
problem was that the second attack almost certainly never happened.
Crewmembers of the Maddox mistook their own sonar pings off the rudder
for North Vietnamese torpedoes.

National Security Agency documents declassified in 2005 show that U.S.
intelligence officials deliberately omitted most of the relevant
communications and that if the reports had been used they would have
shown that no attack happened. A NSA historian wrote that, "A conscious
effort ensued to demonstrate that an attack occurred."

The Navy has concluded that it is "clear that North Vietnamese naval
forces did not attack Maddox and Turner Joy that night."
In private, Johnson expressed doubts about the Gulf of Tonkin incident,
reportedly telling a State Department official that "those dumb, stupid
sailors were just shooting at flying fish!" He also questioned the idea of
being in Vietnam at all. "A man can fight if he can see daylight down the
road somewhere," he told a senator in March 1965. "But there ain't no
daylight in Vietnam, there's not a bit."
Yet even as he said that, he was committing the first ground combat units
and initiating a massive bombing campaign.

On March 8, 1965, 3,500 U.S. Marines became the first American
combat troops to arrive in Vietnam. They landed a few miles east of
downtown Da Nang and the airport at My Khe Beach and joined 23,000
American military advisors in Vietnam.

U.S. Marines land at Da Nang

The beach with 20 miles of white sand would be used by American troops in Vietnam for rest and recreation. The GI's called it "China Beach."

America's treadmill of death was speeding up and the assembly line would feed the war for eight painful, bloody, disastrous years.

U.S. Marines South Vietnam 1968

In 1973, when it finally grounded to a halt, 58,220 U.S. soldiers,

Marines, sailors and airmen's lives' had been lost and 2,500 others would be listed as prisoners, missing in action or killed without their remains being found.

For the thousands of dead and missing, the last friendly American faces they remembered were the pretty flight attendants who smiled at them on the way over.

Chapter 2
The Smiling Faces

Smiles usually came naturally for women who chose to be flight attendants. One of those was 21-year-old Janet Bancroft, a 5' 5," green-eyed California blonde knockout who had always wanted to fly.

Janet Bancroft
1969

Janet started with World Airways in June 1969. "I was in the last class of that year and had attended a two-year college. I hated school and was working in a ski shop in San Mateo, California and on weekends I was a ski instructor at Alpine Meadows in Tahoe. One day a girl came into the shop and we started talking. She was really tan and here it was winter! I asked her how she got her tan and she told me she got it in Australia and was a stew for World."

Janet found out World Airways was based in the Bay Area and they were hiring. Having been turned down by TWA and American Airlines, she hoped things would be different with World and applied.

"I didn't like all of the rioting and peace marches that were going on in schools around the country. I felt very patriotic, so when I found that 60 percent of World's flights were with soldiers, I thought it not only would be fun to see the world, but I would be patriotic as well. A far cry from burning flags!"

Janet liked that flight attendants got a half day off for every day she was gone on a trip and that most trips averaged ten days, leaving her a lot of time to ski when she was home.

She was hired and after completing her training was able to pin on her wings.

* * * * *

In that same June 1969 World Airways flight attendant's class was Fredene Weaver, a 5'5" brown-haired beauty from a small Nevada town with hazel eyes and a quick wit.

Fredene Weaver
1969

From the age of nine, Fredene always wanted to be a stewardess. (Her name was in honor of her father's Navy friend whose first name was Fred and was killed in World War II.)

After graduating from high school, Fredene interviewed with United Airlines but was told they didn't hire anyone until they were 20 and was advised to go to college, which she did and graduated from Santa Clara University. Shortly after that, following a visit with a cousin in Las Vegas, Fredene was on a flight back to San Jose. Seated next to her was Annabelle Pidaloan, who worked for World Airways and said World was hiring. Fredene applied and after persistent phone calls was accepted in the June 1969 training class. Seven weeks later, she pinned on her wings.

World Airways 727

Now married and living in San Luis Obispo, Fredene shared her thoughts with the author on a visit to San Diego.

Fredene Weaver (Maulhardt)
2018

"My first flight was bringing Army troops into Saigon from Japan," she said. "I was the bottom-of-the-ramp girl that day (standing at the bottom of the stairs as troops got off the plane). An 18 or 19-year-old boy . . ." She briefly choked up remembering the moment and continued. "He stopped and he said, 'Can I kiss you? Because I may never come home.'"

Fredene would soon learn that was a standard line from the young men on her flights but she obliged and nearly 50 years later with a sweet laugh said, "They deserved them."

* * * * *

Helen Tennant (Hegelheimer) traced her desire to be a flight attendant from watching television.

"When I was a young gal," she says, "I watched The Mickey Mouse Club and they did a program on what it was like to be a stewardess. I was absolutely glued to the TV set. After that, I cannot remember a time I didn't want to be a stewardess."

Helen Tennant (Hegelheimer) 1966

Helen was born in 1944 in Fontana, California and after graduating from high school in 1962 she briefly attended college before taking a job in 1965 with World Airways, first in administration and then as a flight attendant.

From 1966-1968 she was assigned to transport military personnel in support of the Vietnam War in Southeast Asia.

Her flights originated and terminated at Travis Air Force Base, California and McChord Air Base/Ft. Lewis, Washington. She worked the North Pacific and Mid Pacific routes.

* * * * *

Leslie (Laird) Pfeifer of Moraga, California was a flight attendant with Flying Tiger Line and told her story to Tom Barnidge in an April 26, 2014 article for the Bay Area News Group.

In 1967, interrupting her college career, Leslie became a flight attendant on military transport charters operated by Flying Tiger Line. (She eventually returned to college and received a bachelor's degree.)

She was drawn by the chance to travel the world but could not have pointed out Vietnam on a map.

Leslie Laird (Pfeifer)
1967 Elmendorf AFB, Alaska

Leslie Laird (Pfeifer)
2018

"When I signed on," she said in the article, "I just saw it as a big adventure. I had no idea where Vietnam was. My parents said, 'You're going where? You're doing what?'"

* * * * *

The excitement of flying also appealed to 23-year-old Patti Medaris (now married to the author and looking then like actress Elizabeth Taylor).

Patti Medaris (Culea)
1966

"I used to hang out with fighter pilots at Luke Air Force Base near Phoenix, Arizona. That was 1965 and in 1966 I began dating Lieutenant Joe Adrian. That summer I flew to Illinois to be with my parents before they went to Africa as missionaries. Joe came to visit me on his way home before being deployed to Vietnam.

"After my parents left for Africa, I flew to Los Angeles to work for my uncle who was a heart surgeon and a few months later I was hired at Continental Airlines working as a secretary for the chief flight attendant at Los Angeles International Airport handling the scheduling for flight attendants and spot checks to make sure their weight was in accepted limits. All the airlines had guidelines for weight based on a woman's height. Five or more pounds too much or five or more pounds too little and the flight attendant was put on leave until they could make the standard."

Patti's explanation for the strict physical requirements, length of hair and not allowing flight attendants to be married: "They wanted us to look like the All-American girl."

"The gals would talk about their trips to Vietnam or Japan," Patti said, "and because I had been a stewardess with Bonanza I wanted to get back to flying. A flight attendant told me Flying Tigers was hiring. At the time all the airlines had a height requirement of at least 5'2" and I stood slightly under five feet. But the gal at Continental told me that she thought Tigers might not be so strict so I applied but was rejected by Tigers for being too short. However, I was determined and began calling them once a week on my lunch hour. I said that I realized I was short but I had been a flight attendant with Bonanza and had been on 707's and could reach the overhead racks where the emergency equipment was.

"Finally, I think I wore them down and they called and said, 'OK, Patti here is a date and a time for your interview.'"

So, Patti had her foot in the doorway, however, even though she was long on desire she knew she was literally short on minimum height requirements. But after talking with a friend who said a person's body could be stretched, she called a family friend who was a doctor to see if that were true.

"He said, 'yes, a doctor could add almost an inch but it would last only 3-4 hours.'"

It was just the news Patti needed.

"I called a friend in Oakland (where Flying Tiger Line was based) and asked if she knew a chiropractor close by and she gave me the name and I called and made an appointment for 8:30 the morning of my interview which was two hours later. I flew up there and spent the night with my friend and the next morning was on an examination table. My legs were strapped and after several pulls on my neck, pops in my back and pulls on my head, the session was over. A few steps away, was the height measuring device and ta-da! I was five-feet-one-inch!"

The truth can only be stretched so far and Patti knew that in a few hours, her body would revert to its previous height. So, she high-tailed it for her interview.

"I had the interview first and kept wondering when they would measure how tall I was. Finally, they did and apparently, I measured up to their standards because they hired me on the spot. But I was told I should gain some weight. I was 91 pounds and they said I needed to put on five more pounds."

Next for Patti and all flight attendants were several weeks of intense training of what would be expected of them. Included in the Flying Tiger seven-week course was an understanding that should they be taken hostage by enemy forces, there would be no negotiations for their release.

"I accepted that," she said, "and so did the others, but we really didn't think it would happen."

Having already been through training with Bonanza Airlines, Patti Medaris (Culea) had no problems with what Tigers subjected her to. She remembers one session floating on a raft in San Francisco Bay during emergency evacuation exercises.

"While it was fun, the water was also very cold. I knew if we had to do this in Vietnam, the water would be a lot warmer," she said.

* * * * *

Instructions also included what protection would be given in the combat zone and the locations of bunkers in the event of attack at an airport.

Continental flight attendant Tony Watt
1968

* * * * *

In 1968, Dutch-born Canadian Maureen van Leeuwen (Haldeman) joined Pan Am Flight Service and began her five-week training course. Fortunately, for her and other future Pan Am flight attendants, the water ditching survival training was in a warm swimming pool at the Miami Airways Motel and not in frigid waters of San Francisco Bay. Because almost every flight for Pan Am was over water and the airline did not offer domestic flights, crews had to be strong swimmers.

Miami, Florida 1968
Images courtesy: Everythingpan.com

Maureen and her flight attendant hopefuls were taught cultural customs, and learned to comport themselves. They were schooled in fine wines and how to mix business with pleasure when preparing cocktails. Beyond that they were given the basics in delivering a baby to whipping up a six-course gourmet French meal at 30,000 feet.

Maureen celebrating her new wings with parents Gerald and Kathleen van Leeuwen 1968
Images courtesy: Everythingpanam.com

Maureen, fluent in French, Dutch, German and English was with Pan Am from April 1968 until the end of 1971 with much of the time transporting troops to and from Vietnam.

Maureen van Leeuwen (Haldeman)
Images courtesy: Everythingpanam.com

* * * * *

During her training, the Pan Am women would have heard the same thing that Patti Medaris (Culea) was told in her Flying Tiger Line classes. "Our trainer told us we needed to know emergency procedures better than our names," Patti remembers. "We had first aid classes, how to deploy the chutes and how to jump and slide down the chutes. We jumped out of a real plane on the tarmac, not a simulator and did it several times. We learned how to deploy life rafts and while floating around the bay find the necessary equipment in the raft which included desalination kits, C-rations, first aid kits, blankets, a canopy to keep the sun away, flare guns and ELT's (Emergency Locater Transmitter). Also on the rafts were Gideon bibles."

Before they could begin their overseas assignment, Patti and other flight attendants became human pincushions. They were on the firing line at Travis Air Force Base for all sorts of immunizations.

"Sometimes they had regular hypodermic needles," Patti remembers, "but other times they used 'guns' on us."

I. INTERNATIONAL CERTIFICATES OF VACCINATION

AS APPROVED BY

THE WORLD HEALTH ORGANIZATION

(EXCEPT FOR ADDRESS OF VACCINATOR)
CERTIFICATS INTERNATIONAUX DE VACCINATION
APPROUVÉS PAR
L'ORGANISATION MONDIALE DE LA SANTÉ
(SAUF L'ADRESSE DU VACCINATEUR)

II. PERSONAL HEALTH HISTORY

TRAVELER'S NAME—Nom du voyageur

Patti Medaris

ADDRESS   (Number—Numéro)   (Street—Rue)
ADRESSE

770 W. Imperial Ave. #30

(City—Ville)

El Segundo, Calif.

(County—Département)   (State—État)

U.S. DEPARTMENT OF
HEALTH, EDUCATION, AND WELFARE

PUBLIC HEALTH SERVICE

PHS–731   READ CAREFULLY
Rev. 9–66   INSTRUCTIONS
                 Pages 10 and 11

INTERNATIONAL CERTIFICATE OF VACCINATION OR REVACCINATION AGAINST CHOLERA
CERTIFICAT INTERNATIONAL DE VACCINATION OU DE REVACCINATION CONTRE LE CHOLÉRA

This is to certify that   sex   F
Je soussigné(e) certifie que   sexe

whose signature follows   Patricia Medaris   date of birth   Nov. 7, 1942
dont la signature suit   né(e) le

has on the date indicated been vaccinated or revaccinated against cholera.
a été vacciné(e) ou revacciné(e) contre le choléra à date indiquée.

Date	Signature, professional status, and address of vaccinator / Signature, qualité professionnelle, et adresse du vaccinateur	Approved stamp / Cachet d'authentification
1. 16-Oct-6 / OCT 3 0 1967	H.R. Frierson, M.D. / 915 N. Sepulveda / El Segundo, Calif.	VACCINATION SC 293 USA
2. 2 0 MAY 1970	Major, USAF, MC. / Travis Air Force Base, / California, USA 94535	

Date	Vaccine	Dose	Physician's Signature
9/oct/67	Typhoid #1	0.5cc	H. R. Frierson, M.D.
25/Sept/67	Jet Inj (B)	0.5cc	H. R. Frierson, M.D.
13/oct/67	Plague #1	0.5cc	H. R. Frierson, M.D.
16-Oct-67	Typhus #1	1cc	H.R Frierson, M.D.
11-Nov-67	Typhoid #2	0.5cc	JACK E. KAHOUN, M.D.
11-Nov-67	Plague #2	0.5cc	JACK E. KAHOUN, M.D.
20 MAY 1970	Plague	(B)	RONALD S GREEN, USAF [MC]

On October 27, 1967, Patti received her wings from Flying Tiger Line along with a GS (General Schedule)-11 designation, the military equivalent of an Army Captain. Her pay was about $400 a month.

Patti's Flying Tiger uniform

After she was hired, Patti was given an identification card. That card had to be turned in when she left Flying Tiger Line, however, in 1970 when she went to work for Airlift International, the identification card they gave her never was turned in because she was furloughed in 1971.

I. D. CARD No. 4399

AIRLIFT
INTERNATIONAL, INC.
EXECUTIVE OFFICES - MIAMI, FLA.

Patricia M. Medaris
NAME
1653 West Missouri
HOME ADDRESS
Phoenix   Arizona
CITY   STATE
Flight Attendant
POSITION/JOB   EMPLOYEE NO.

11/07/42	U.S.
DATE OF BIRTH	CITIZENSHIP
Female	5'1"
SEX	HEIGHT
105	Green
WEIGHT	EYES
Brown	
HAIR	SOCIAL SECURITY No.
A Positive	None
BLOOD TYPE	ALLERGIES

EMPLOYEE'S SIGNATURE

THIS CARD IS NOT TRANSFERABLE AND MUST BE SUR-
RENDERED TO THE COMPANY ON TERMINATION OF EM-
PLOYMENT.

Technically speaking she is still with the CIA-fronted airline and while the CIA specialized in deep intelligence, as you can see, Patti pulled a fast one on the spook airline and listed herself as 5' 1"—a stretch of her imagination and wishful thinking.

* * * * *

Another flight attendant for Airlift International was Gretchen Bergstresser (Garren).

Gretchen Bergstresser (Garren) 1967-1968

While Patti Medaris (Culea) finagled her way past the height requirement to join Airlift, even though you had to be 21 to work for the airline, Gretchen was just 18 when she filled out her application.

"I always had to make excuses not to go down to the bar with the crew," she says. " No one knew my age at the time. I considered everything with the airline a big adventure," Gretchen writes 51 years later. She tried her best to comfort troops that had been wounded.

"Whenever we would land at a base we always asked if there was a MEDIVAC flight on the ground," she remembers. "We would board the plane and ask everyone their name and where they were from. We always tried to make light of their injuries and engage them in conversation. We often wondered if they survived and were able to go home."

Gretchen 1967   Gretchen 2018

On a particularly harrowing night in 1968, she remembers having doubts if she would make it out alive.

"I recall one time we were ferrying the airplane into Ben Hoa during the Tet Offensive and the captain came out and told us a missile had hit the airport terminal and asked us if we wanted to go back. He said the troops there were waiting to hear back from us if we were coming. 'Hell yes,' was our answer, we had to get those guys out of there. When we landed, they put the stairs up to the plane and I went down to the bottom of the stairs on the ramp. We had 15 minutes to board about 120 guys and get back in the air. When I looked down the ramp all the soldiers were lined up and ready to board. We kept the aircraft engines running and I said, 'Okay lets go, we have to get out of here.' It was pitch dark and when they came running toward the plane I realized they all were carrying their rifles and we couldn't allow them on the plane. An order was given and 120 rifles hit the ground. It was amazing to see these guys climb up the stairs and run to the back of the plane and get into their seats and be ready to go. The whole plane rocked back and forth as they ran to their seats. The last one was up the stairs with me right behind him and we closed the doors, taxied out and were airborne without incident. Can you imagine being sitting ducks out there with our plane cabin lights the only visible target expecting an attack at any moment? No one said a word until wheels up and then everyone cheered. Great trip."

* * * * *

JoAnn Wright (Wintenburg) had her sights set on flying from an early age.

"I knew I wanted to be a flight attendant in my senior year of high school during a vocational training class," she says, "yet I had never been in an airplane. If I didn't fly then I planned to go to school to become a beautician. You had to be 20 to fly and I got hired while I was still 19 but graduated from training four days after I turned 20."

JoAnn Wright (Wintenburg)
1967

JoAnn's first base was Dallas and then when Continental opened

Houston she moved there. It was a good move for her since few flight attendants elected to bid for that base and she ended up being a senior #5 after flying for only five months.

Then after eight months, Military Airlift Command (MAC) trips opened up and JoAnn, homesick for her home in Los Angeles, signed on and was transferred there.

"I was a bit ignorant about what I was getting in to when I bid MAC," JoAnn recalls. "At age 21, I was the youngest person at Continental flying MAC and was not in touch with my mortality. I look back at that with amazement. I could relate to the military guys because most of them were about my age coming out of boot camp. They were scared and exhausted and slept most of the way over wondering if they were going to come home dead or alive. Most all of them smoked and after the meals, the smoke was so thick that you could hardly see the other end of the cabin. Then they would all go back to sleep, only getting up to use the restrooms."

JoAnn would be on MAC flights to and from Vietnam from April 1968 to 1972.

JoAnn Wright (Wittenberg) 1967

* * * * *

In the late 1960's, all across the country, women like JoAnn were answering the call to join airlines that couldn't hire flight attendants fast enough.

Pan American World Airways was arguably the most prestigious and difficult airline to land a job as a flight attendant. There were reports that out of every 50,000 women interviewed, only 500 were chosen.

The 1967 *Time* magazine ad gave the benefits and what was needed to come on board. Pan Am offered up to $550 a month salary after three years, thirty days paid vacation a year, up to 90% discounts off vacation travel and all expenses paid while away from home base. Requirements were strict; applicants had to be single, over 21, between 5'3" and 5'9." They had to be at least a high school graduate and a second language was mandatory.

* * * * *

A long-time member of the Continental Airlines team was flight attendant Bea Weber, hired in 1957 at age of 21. Born in Albuquerque, New Mexico, she would fly for Continental on Military Airlift Command flights eight years from August 1964 to August 1972 and then continue with Continental another 30 years.

In 2019 at age 83, in a telephone interview from her home in Scottsdale, Arizona, Bea shared memorable moments of her 45-year career at Continental. One of them was the story behind the photo below showing Bea and a soldier with his drug-sniffing German Shepherd.

Bea Weber at Tai Son Naut Airfield in Saigon

It turns out the soldier was there to find out if Bea had any extra ham and cheese sandwiches on the plane. For the soldier? Nope. The dog loved them.

* * * * *

In 2018, John Ruch, writing for Reporter Newspapers, tells the adventures of Joan Policastro who signed on in 1968 as a Pan American World Airways flight attendant.

Joan Policastro
Photo from: Reporter Newspapers

"Joan had graduated from the University of Miami and wanted to attend law school, but was short on money. She had seen and heard Pan Am ads offering the job of stewardesses. Their standards were high, a four-year degree and the ability to speak at least one language besides English. She measured up and decided to try it for a year. The year would eventually turn into 50 with the first four spent flying 'rest and recuperation' flights with U.S. troops in and out of the Vietnam War.

"'I liked it. I liked them,' said Joan 'Everybody on the airplane was a baby,' she says. 'I was 22. They looked 12.'

"There were times when they landed that airports were under attack.

"'I never worried about that,' she said. 'It's the luck of the draw.'"

"'Pan Am offered the chartered flights to the U.S. military at cost plus $1,'" she said. "'In return, all crew got Department of Defense ID cards giving them an honorary lieutenant's rank — possibly ensuring better treatment if they were shot down and captured. Back in those days, when you had any connection with the U.S. military, you felt safe,' she said.

"'On one midnight landing at Cam Rahn Bay, Joan could see and hear bombs in the distance,' directed at the base. She said an officer came on board and told the troops, 'When you get 50 feet off the airplane, hit the ground.'"

Ruch's story concluded with, "Joan continued to fly with Pan Am until the company's dissolution in 1991. She then joined Delta and retired in 2018."

* * * * *

In January 2019, the author spoke with Policastro by telephone from her Georgia home.

While she values her 27 years with Delta, she will always think of herself as a Pan Am person.

"No matter how good an airline Delta was, nothing and I mean nothing compares to what Pan Am was," she says emphatically and with emotion. "It was a great airline to work for."

* * * * *

In 1969, Marsha May (Merz) was a patriotic 21-year-old college student looking for travel and adventure with a desire to serve her country. She signed on with Flying Tiger Line and after completing ground school and having her first check ride, the next week she was working a Military Airlift Command trip to Vietnam. Little did she know that she would be with the airline for the next 23 years.

Marsha May (Merz) second from bottom step 1970

She remembers in 1969 Flying Tigers had a large fleet of stretch DC-8's and four of them were configured for military passenger flights, each with 219 seats.

The routes carrying U.S. military personnel usually were between McChord Air Force Base or Travis Air Force Base to Vietnam with stops in Anchorage Alaska and Yokota Air Force Base, Japan for fuel, food and a fresh crew. The final destination in Vietnam was usually Cam Rahn Bay, Saigon or Da Nang.

"Our passenger flights," she remembers, "were scheduled to land and takeoff during daylight hours. To be safe, we did not layover in Vietnam and passenger planes were only on the ground for a few hours; just long enough to disembark passengers, refuel and clean the interior of the aircraft and then load the plane with our homeward bound G.I.'s.

"To ensure a short ground time in Vietnam, all of our meals for trips into and out of the country were loaded into our galleys in Yokota, Japan. We served 219 hot meals from Japan to Vietnam and 219 more hot meals flying back from Vietnam to Japan, which meant our galleys were packed extremely tight."

* * * * *

Another young woman answering the call to join the airlines was 24-year-old BJ Elliott (Prior) who found herself in a four-week training class for Continental Airlines in Los Angeles.

In her book *Behind My Wings*, BJ tells of being in a class with 41 other women, some with checkered backgrounds and lifestyles. One discovered she was pregnant during training and had to leave. At that time, flight attendants could not be married or have children. Flight attendants of that era say the airlines wanted them to look like the "All American girl."

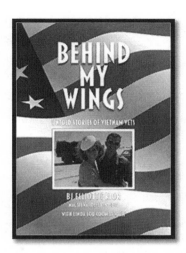

Book cover and photos courtesy BJ Elliott (Prior)

BJ's class began with 42 young women but at the end, eleven had dropped out for reasons that included refusing to have their hair cut short and above the collar.

BJ Elliott (Prior) (Second from the left)

She graduated as a flight attendant and for the next nine months, BJ flew domestically for Continental but soon was spending too much time in the lavatory throwing up. On short flights, especially going into Denver,

Colorado the turbulence was so severe it made her airsick. She thought of quitting but then heard about Continental's military flights to transport troops to Vietnam and she signed up.

On March 8, 1969, seated on a jump seat inside a 707 and facing 165 soldiers, BJ made her initial flight to Vietnam; first stop, Honolulu and to her great relief she did not get sick on descent. After a layover, several days later, she arrived in Vietnam.

BJ Elliott (Prior) (middle)

* * * * *

Lorna McLearie sneaked in under the age door at World Airways in 1970 and was hired as a flight attendant two months shy of turning 21. She would be with World for 17 years.

Lorna McLearie getting her wings at graduation 1970

"It was a job many of our generation wanted because of the travel," she said. "Much better than backpacking and riding in a VW van, which was the common vehicle at the time.

"I chose World because their only base was Oakland and I wanted to stay in California. I did not realize I would have a nomad existence with constant schedule changes.

One day I would be in Paris working a charter flight and another day returning to the Far East and Vietnam."

Lorna, who went on to become an interior designer and lives in Napa, California, remembers her first trip with World.

"It was an exciting journey to Amsterdam and then Spain before returning to New York. And then came Vietnam."

"My second trip with World I was alerted I would be based in Japan for one month, flying Saigon turns. We stayed at the Airline Hotel outside of the Yokota airbase. The hotel was filled with crews flying in and out of Saigon but also Korean trips and to the states."

Lorna McLearie (center)

"Being raised Catholic I always said, 'Hail Mary's' and 'Our Fathers' on take offs and landings."

"I did not grow up oblivious to the pain and loss of war. My mother lost her first husband in World War II when my older sister was only 2 months old. This kind of loss effects generations. I always felt we never belonged in Vietnam and was conflicted.

"The common route for World Airways was Saigon, Yokota Air Base, Japan, Anchorage and then Fairfield, California. Crews were then bused back to Oakland airport. We would all sign out at dispatch and check our mailboxes for airline memos and notes from friends.

"I lived in Marin county most of the time and spent much time at the ocean on my days off. It was a time before cell phones, computers, but we had poetry readings, art exhibits and long conversations in North Beach until our coffee went cold."

* * * * *

In 1961, 21-year-old Lydia Cowgill had just graduated from Los Angeles Trade Technical College with an associate degree in art, but needed to find a job that paid more than what her field of study could provide.

"I looked at the classified ads and saw that United Airlines was conducting interviews," she said.

Lydia went for the interview and was hired by United but a year later joined Flying Tiger Line.

In a 2019 interview from her Fallbrook, California home, Lydia spoke with the author and his wife, Patti who also flew with Flying Tiger Line in 1967 but did not know Lydia at the time.

Lydia Rossi and Patti Culea 2019

In 1961, after Lydia was hired by United and completed her training in Chicago, she was based in Newark, New Jersey. During that time, she received a post card from a woman in her United training class who quit and had gone to work for Flying Tiger Line. The post card was from Tahiti, a bit more glamorous than Newark.

"I'd never been anywhere," Lydia said, "and grew up near Burbank and saw Flying Tiger signs and their planes on the tarmac."

This was in 1963. A week after she applied, she was hired by Flying Tigers.

Lydia's training took all of six hours and after being measured and fitted for a custom uniform, the next day she was on a plane walking the aisle. Since she had been through United's training, the short session wasn't a problem but there were several newly hired women in her class who had not worked for other airlines.

In an understatement she says, "They didn't have a succinct training then."

Lydia's first flight into Vietnam was in 1965 when American troop strength began increasing. On board the Canadair CL-44 was a planeload of young Army soldiers.

"On final approach," she remembers, "I could see them praying and taking out their rosaries. They were scared."

That night, Lydia and the crew stayed at the Caravelle Hotel.

Caravelle Hotel, Saigon 1965

On future flights into Vietnam, unless there were mechanical problems, Flying Tiger Line would not have planes and employees remain overnight in country. However, on this occasion, Lydia carries a memory of her meal that night.

"Our senior flight attendant thought my friend and I were kind of green, so she says, 'Alright, everybody come up to the rooftop and we're going to have a drink and dinner.'"

Lydia Cowgill (Rossi)
Caravelle Hotel roof, Saigon 1965

"'You're all going to order escargot,' our supervisor said."
"We were like, 'What's escargot?'"
"We ordered it and we liked it."

* * * * *

Months later, Lydia would make another trip into Saigon with troops, this time on a 707 and then fly out to the Philippines the next day. The pilot on that flight would eventually become her husband as will be told later in Chapter 10.

* * * * *

If one had to choose flight attendants who could be considered legends, beside Joan Policastro, the list would have to include Jeannie Wagers (Wiseman) who joined World Airways in 1962.

Jeannie Wagers (Wiseman)
Late 1960's Saigon

Even today, former flight attendants who worked under her supervision remember how intimidating she could be. She ran things by the "book" and referred to the women she supervised as "my beanies." Some women thought the term was degrading but were afraid to ask her what she meant. Writing to the author, Jeannie explained, "*Beanies* are in reference to the hats we wore. Matching the uniform in a wheat color they were like a baseball hat only very tall with a narrow brim."

The uniform change in 1968

Fredene Weaver (Maulhardt) 1969 and a 1970 "Beanie"

At World Airways, potential flight attendants learned quickly they
needed to look and dress a certain way. Helen Tennant (Hegelheimer) said,
"We had extremely strict rules about our appearance. Everybody had to look
exactly the same. We even had to wear the same fingernail polish and the
same kind of perfume. We weren't allowed to wear earrings and our hair
had to be short or at least worn up. You couldn't look provocative in our
uniforms."

Helen Tennant (Hegelheimer) 1966

"They were very tailored, sort of Jackie Kennedy-like camelhair suits.

The skirts were mid-knee even though it was the sixties. The most distinctive thing was our polo hat with this huge crown on it."

* * * * *

Lorna McLearie writes, "The tailors who did our uniforms hemmed mine too short, which I had nothing to do with--Lili Ann Designs. I was only 20 and often was asked if I was old enough to be flying. It was like a military school for me. We had a strict dress code for our time on base and in uniform we could never chew gum. I do not like gum, so no loss."

* * * * *

Several flight attendants interviewed for this book remembered having to wear girdles. Said Patti Medaris (Culea), "Nothing was to wiggle."

And one flight attendant said that the later World Airways polyester uniform had the colors of A &W Root Beer.

* * * * *

In 2018 the author and his wife, Patti (the former Flying Tiger Line flight attendant mentioned earlier) met Jeannie Wagers (Wiseman) at her San Diego home.

Jeannie Wagers (Wiseman) and Patti Medaris (Culea)

Then 84, Jeannie talked about the World Airline flight attendant's uniform. Some said the hats resembled a billed pumpkin. "Go ahead and laugh," she says, "but back in '66 that outfit was the cat's meow. Stews from other airlines would come up and say, 'What a wonderful uniform!'"

World Airways graduation class October 1965

* * * * *

The look may have been stylish, but the material was another story, especially to Flying Tiger Line flight attendants. Patti Medaris (Culea) questioned the sanity of those who chose the uniform fabric.

"I can't believe that they made us wear heavy wool uniforms, especially working in the stifling heat of Vietnam or the Philippines."

Flying Tiger Line uniforms late 1960's
Courtesy FlyingTigerLine.org
"The Way It Was"

Flying Tiger Line crew having a flat tire changed on their way from San Francisco to Travis Air Force Base (the flight attendants are wearing their wool uniforms) 1968

* * * * *

When World Airways began carrying troops into Vietnam and Jeannie was given her Department of Defense identification card, she quickly learned that her life would be more than being on the war's fringes.

"Someone told me," she said, "if you're captured and you show it (the ID card) to the Viet Cong, they will nail it to your forehead."

* * * * *

Janet Bancroft (Burttram) remembers her first flight into Cam Ranh Bay. "I sent my parents a postcard and told them there really was a war going on when I saw the soldiers lined up with guns behind sand bag bunkers as we taxied to the Quonset hut terminal."

* * * * *

JoAnn Wright (Wintenburg) remembers having to carry her immunization record along with her passport.

"All crew members got Department of Defense cards," she says, "which I wish I could have kept that but if we did not return them it was a $100 fine, which was a lot in those days. It showed flight attendants as a 2nd lieutenant with the Air Force in case of our capture. That got my attention."

* * * * *

Caution of another kind involved some of what flight attendants saw. For Patti Medaris (Culea) it was a top-secret spy plane.

"While I was with Flying Tigers at Kadena Air Force Base in Japan, I was on an airplane early helping set up the galley. While waiting for the food truck to arrive I was standing in the open doorway and saw an amazing plane taxi and then take off in seconds! It was the XB-71 Valkyrie spy plane!"

"I was thrilled but later that evening after our return from Vietnam I was told not to say anything about what I had seen. They said we were not supposed to know where our spy planes were based."

Chapter 3
The Airlines

There were about twenty airlines that contracted with the U.S. government to fly troops in and out of the Vietnam War. The flights were called Military Airlift Command or better known as MAC flights. Some airlines were well known like United, TWA, Pan Am, Braniff, Continental and Northwest while others carried not-so-familiar names such as Trans International Airlines, Capitol Airways, Seaboard World, Flying Tiger Line, World Airways, Saturn, Universal, Air Vietnam and Overseas National Airways.

For Overseas National Airways 60% of its revenue was generated from military contracts. And there were still others with shadowy ownership.

Several of those were fronts for the United States Central Intelligence Agency (CIA) and included Southern Air Transport and as mentioned in the previous chapter, Airlift International.

Airlift International 727

Another was Air America that began prior to World War II when the American government sent General Claire L. Chennault and his rag-tag commandos to China. They flew P-40 fighters against the Japanese Air Force during the fight for the Chinese mainland.

Air America DC-6A/B 1968

After the war, the American government formed Civil Air Transport (CAT), a fleet of aircraft that supported Chinese Nationalists. At one time it was the largest "airline" in the world.

Then in the 1960's when things got dicey in Laos, Cambodia and Vietnam, the CIA merged its "airlines" under the name of Air America and recruited hot-shot civilian pilots and crew members. Most were mercenary airmen from the American military.

* * * * *

George Gewehr, a pilot for Flying Tiger Line during the Vietnam War and current historian for the Flying Tiger Line Pilots' Association explained the complicated business arrangement that existed between the government and airlines that transported troops during the war.

Flying Tiger DC-8-63

George Gewehr in 1994 and today

"The basic contracts ran anywhere from $60 million and up," he said. "In 1967 to operate a DC-8-63, which was the largest one then, it cost $2,654 per hour for a round trip of 26 hours flown. That included the crew, fuel, maintenance and insurance costs."

(Note: The so-called "stretch" DC-8 could carry about 221 passengers compared with about 150 in a Boeing 727 but at a cost of only about 10 percent more than the smaller aircraft.)

There were two routes the airlines took to transport troops and it depended on the time of year. The northern route went through Alaska and Japan while the southern route went through Hawaii or in some cases, straight to Japan.

Gewehr continues. "If you flew from Seattle to Anchorage to Yokota, and down to Vietnam it would take about 26 hours, maybe less. If we calculated the whole time taken to do it times the cost it would be $69,004. The company was paid $100,000 per round trip. So there was a profit of $30,996 per trip."

The pay range for flight attendants to the flight crew was wide. Flight attendant Fredene (Weaver) Maulhardt remembers clearing $398 a month not counting per diem.

George Gewehr says, "The captain's pay was $68.70 per hour, the copilot $47.50 per hour and the flight engineer $35 per hour. Per Diem for the flight crew was $1.30 an hour. This was paid only on a layover on a trip."

Flying Tiger Line had 270 pilots (135 captains and 135 copilots). There were 154 flight engineers and 85 navigators for a total aircrew of 509.

Tigers had approximately 320 stewardesses (later called flight attendants) during the Vietnam War. There were no male flight attendants at Tigers then; they came after the war ended.

* * * * *

Perhaps the most charismatic owner of any airline that flew during the Vietnam War was Edward Daly who bought World Airways in 1950 for $50,000.

Ed Daly with flight attendants (Janet Bancroft (Burttram) is second from right)

Daly's generosity was legendary, personally funding circus trips for 5,000 Oakland children every year, Ice Follies tickets for 2,000 and Nutcracker ballet tickets for 1,000. The one-time Golden Gloves boxer built a swimming pool for a county ward and supported at least one orphanage in Vietnam.

World Airways flight attendant Janet Bancroft (Burttram) at a Catholic orphanage sponsored by Ed Daly

Daly is best remembered for what happened starting on March 26, 1975 when World began flying refugees out of Da Nang to Saigon. Daly oversaw the evacuation of 2,000 people over two days. The efforts cost Daly millions of dollars and almost his life as told by writer Larry Englelmann on March 24, 2017 in *Vietnam Magazine* and shown on *The History Channel*.

Each flight was a harrowing experience with mobs of people clamoring to get on the plane that was designed to carry 131 passengers.

On March 28, citing increased danger, the U.S. Embassy suspended flights in favor of an international seaborne rescue operation. Daly objected and moved forward to save women and children in what would be billed as the "last flight from Da Nang".

In Saigon, Daly rounded up his crew; World Airways Chief Pilot, 52-year-old Ken Healy, co-pilot Glen Flansaas and flight engineer Charles Stewart. Jan Wollett was the senior flight attendant.

Jan Wollett World Airways Flight Attendant 1975

Two other flight attendants on board were Valerie Witherspoon and, on her first flight for World, 21-year-old Atsako Okuba. Also along for the harrowing ride were television network crews including reporter Bruce Dunning from CBS.

When the 727 taxied on the Saigon runway, air traffic controllers ordered the pilot to stop and return to the hanger. Daly told his pilot to experience "radio failure" and the plane sped past the terminal and took off.

An hour and twenty minutes later, as the 727 touched down in Da Nang, thousands of people raced from the hangars and other buildings toward the aircraft while it was taxiing.

Suddenly, a new Ford Mustang raced down the runway driven by a 19-year-old Vietnamese Air Force military policeman. The car was to be delivered to the local military police chief's commander who had deserted. In the car were the driver's 16-year-old girlfriend and another man.

The driver pulled his car ahead of the plane and then got out and fired a pistol in the air just over the cockpit to get the pilot to stop. The man remembered looking directly into the pilot's eyes and also seeing a flight attendant standing behind the pilot looking down at him.

The plane did not stop, so the man with gun got back in the car and with tires spinning and smoking, the Mustang roared back into the infield. The plane passed the car and behind the Mustang, thousands of desperate people were running to the 727.

Finally, the plane stopped and the air stair was lowered. The rush of people was terrifying, more so because nearly all of those clamoring to get on board were armed and desperate deserting Vietnamese soldiers. The soldiers were from South Vietnam's so-called toughest unit, the First Division's Black Panthers. A grenade detonated under the plane but the aircraft was not seriously damaged.

As flight engineer Steward and attendant Witherspoon pulled people through the entrance, they kept screaming, "Where are the women and children?"

Senior flight attendant Jan Wollett saw Ed Daly at the bottom of the air stair being mauled by soldiers trying to get on the plane. The deserting soldiers had abandoned their wives and children and were clawing their way to get on the plane. One soldier kicked an old woman in the face to get on board.

Crowds of soldiers fought to get on but Daly, an ex-boxer, emptied his pistol in the air and used his fists in a futile attempt to keep soldiers from displacing women and children. At one point when flight attendants Wollett and Witherspoon pulled a woman over the side of the air stair, a soldier yanked the woman away and as she fell, he stepped on her back and head to get up the railing. Wollett said that when Ed Daly saw that happen, he smashed the soldier in the head with his pistol. The man fell off and was trampled under the feet of the mob.

Ed Daly March 29, 1975

Despite his best efforts Daly could not restore order and was injured trying to stop Vietnamese soldiers from getting on the plane. Finally, with the aircraft dangerously overloaded, it started its takeoff roll with the 727's back air stairs still down and Daly fending off additional people trying get on the plane. Another grenade went off under the left wing destroying the aileron controls on that side. When the crew raised the ladder they were attacked with bullets and grenades. The plane hurtled forward but pilot Healy misjudged the distance between the runway and three nearby sheds. His left wing sliced through all three buildings causing his control panel to flash wildly. When he tried to point the nose up, the controls pulled back. Healy did not know the wheel wells were filled with people, clinging to the cables. When the wheel well opened, some people, unable to hold on to the plane, fell to their death.

Sadly only five women and three children made it on board and regard Daly as the sole figure who helped them to freedom. The rest of the men who forced their way on the plane were some of the soldiers whom South Vietnam President Nguyen Van Thieu said would defend Da Nang.

Ed Daly and Captain Ken Healy

When the airplane landed at Saigon there were 250 people in the main cabin, an estimated 80 packed into the baggage compartment and an additional 24 had been in the two wheel wells (although all but seven had fallen out when the bottom of the wheel wells opened after takeoff). The mangled body of one soldier, his rifle still strapped to his shoulder, was removed from the undercarriage of the 727.

There were four men in the cockpit, including Daly, three flight attendants, five journalists and Joe Hrezo, one of World's station managers, for a total of 367 people on board—nearly three times the capacity. The deserting troops who had stormed the plane were arrested.

When Captain Healy gave Boeing the estimated weight and number of passengers, Boeing's engineers said it was impossible for a 727 so overloaded to take off. All Healy said was, "You build one hell of an airplane."

Operations Babylift and Orphan Airlift

Four days later, Ed Daly's World Airways planned another flight to rescue helpless children from Vietnam.

Instrumental in pulling it off was Charles Patterson a highly decorated Army soldier in World War II who had been with World Airways as a vice president and head of public affairs since 1968.

Charles Patterson

Daly passed a telex to Patterson from his daughter, Charlotte stating that help was needed to get orphans out of South Vietnam before the country fell.

World Airways had a DC-8 it was using to fly rice to Cambodia but had to be flown back to the U.S. for a maintenance check. It was in cargo configuration but Patterson and Daly agreed it could be used to carry the children. Daly said it would be turned into a "flying crib."

Cardboard boxes were fashioned into cribs and cargo nets were put in place to secure the children inside the plane. After some delays, the plane, piloted by Ken Healy, the same man who flew the World Airways 727 out of Da Nang readied the DC-8 for takeoff.

Ken Healy

The runway lights were turned off. Some think because of a possible Viet Cong attack, others are convinced because the plane didn't have clearance to take off it was the U.S. government trying to slow down Daly's babylift. Eyewitnesses say air traffic controllers in the tower were screaming at the pilots to return.

Aboard as a flight attendant was Jan Wollett who had also been on the famed "Last Flight out of Da Nang" mentioned earlier.

JanWollett 1975   Jan Wollett 2015
Credit KUOW photo/Isolde Raftery

In an excellent April 28, 1975 article for *The American Homefront Project*, Wollett told writer Patricia Murphy what happened.

"He (pilot Healy) hit every light he had on the Stretch 8, and we barreled down a dark runway and took off," she says.

Wollett had lined the floor of the plane with blankets because it had no seats. During takeoff, every adult had their arms around the youngest children, she says.

"The ones that were older would snuggle close to you, but they could hold on," she says. "I'd put their little bodies underneath so they would always be protected."

Once airborne, Wollett says she and other flight attendants turned the plane into a giant playpen.

Flight Attendants Valarie Witherspoon (seated) and Carol Shabata (standing)

"Especially when the sun came up and it was daylight and they could see out and see the ocean, and every once and a while you might see a ship and they'd get all excited," Wollett says. "So they were kind of enjoying whatever they could, and we were loving them. So it was pretty great."

The DC-8 made it to Yokota, Japan and then flew to Oakland, California where Ed Daly's daughter Charlotte met it along with doctors who had arranged to take the youngsters to the Sixth Army headquarters.

* * * * *

The next day, President Gerald Ford announced that the U.S. would officially begin to evacuate orphaned babies and children from Saigon. Thousands of children would be airlifted from Vietnam and adopted by families around the world including the United States, France, Australia, West Germany and Canada. The mass evacuation was called Operation Babylift with the first flight scheduled for April 4, 1975 from Saigon to the Philippines. From there the orphans were to be put on charter flights and taken to San Diego where President Ford would meet them.

Good intentions turned tragic. On that first flight fifteen minutes after takeoff from Saigon with 226 orphans on board, a cargo door on the U.S. Air Force C-5A blew out and cut control cables and hydraulic lines. The pilot tried to return the plane to the runway but on final approach the plane landed in a rice paddy, bellied on the ground, skidded and broke apart. Of 330 people aboard, 135 were killed, including 76 of the 226 orphans on their way to an adoption agency in Colorado.

At the same time artillery attacks by North Vietnamese Army units and the Viet Cong were increasing on Tan Son Nhut Air Base at Saigon, so further evacuations were halted.

That's when American businessman Robert Macauley stepped in.

Robert Macauley
Image from: Bangor Daily News

Macauley's Shoeshine Boys Foundation helped feed and clothe war orphans and some were on the plane that crashed. After learning there were no military transport planes to evacuate the surviving orphans, Macauley contacted Pan Am and arranged for 300-orphaned children to leave the country. He didn't have the $10,000 down payment to charter a plane, so he wrote a bad check to get the Pan Am 747 in the air. He later mortgaged his Connecticut home to cover the entire $251,000 cost of the flight from Saigon to San Francisco.

* * * * *

On board many of the evacuation flights were passengers who were pregnant. World Airways flight attendant Jeannie Wagers (Wiseman) remembers being in Honolulu when a flight arrived from Vietnam with refugees. During the trip a woman gave birth to a baby.

The new mother was put on a stretcher and carried off the plane while a flight attendant held a blanketed bundle in her arms that contained the baby. Behind her another flight attendant carried a sack containing the after birth.

An example of how strict the airline was with paper work, Jeannie remembered thinking, "How do you show one more arriving than got on at the origin."

Jeannie says the crew was allowed to stay over in Honolulu to visit the baby. And she says the World Airways captain marked a map for the family with the baby's arrival point between islands.

* * * * *

Photographs show Jeannie and others on evacuation flights that brought orphans to their new families.

* * * * *

Another perspective of World Airways owner Ed Daly comes from
Jeannie.

Jeannie Wagers (Wiseman)

"He was brilliant and could be a real jerk. Take your pick," she says seated in her kitchen and waits for her bluntness to sink in.

"Some people thought he set the moon," she says but recalled another episode that was less than inspiring. "One day Daly got on the plane's PA and was half drunk. I ran to the cockpit and said, 'Pull the circuit breakers,' and then I ran through the cabin saying, 'that wasn't the captain, that wasn't the captain!'"

* * * * *

Daly had his own personal plane, a twin engine prop-driven light green Convair 580 with a shamrock on the tail and a dancing leprechaun painted near the side door.

"I was assigned to the pickle (nickname for the plane) once," Jeannie remembers. He always had his personal flight attendants with him, frequently Filipino girls who didn't get paid but were on expense accounts and could charge just about anything."

Janet Bancroft (Burttram) and unidentified flight attendant on Edward Daly's "pickle"

   In the photo above, Janet Bancroft (Burttram) recalled flying with Ed Daly on several occasions.
   "He drove a Lamborghini and lived life large. I remember a couple of trips with him; one was to many bases in South Vietnam including Pleiku, which was smack dab in the thick of things. The officers hosted lunch for our crew and others on the plane."
   That memory was better than her first encounter with the boss in 1971 while on a trip to Hong Kong where Daly was trying to have World Airways become the first U.S carrier into Mainland China.
   "I was serving him a cup of coffee while we were taxiing for takeoff (he was in the lavatory shaving)," she said. "I poured the coffee in a paper coffee cup for safety reasons since we were moving but was told with no misunderstanding that in the future to always serve him food and beverage on china."

Janet's flying partner on that trip was flight attendant Fredene Weaver (Maulhardt). They spent a week in Hong Kong with all expenses paid by Ed Daly.

Ed Daly in Hong Kong with Fredene Weaver (Maulhardt) and Janet Bancroft (Burttram) (1971)

Daly did not win the Mainland China contract, one of the few things in life that eluded him.

Ed Daly
* * * * *

For Patti Medaris (Culea), major challenges in the air came from military dependents, usually wives and their children who were flying to R & R destinations to meet up with spouses.

One flight from Anchorage to Kadena was so memorable she remembers the exact date, December 18, 1967.

"I understood that the spouses and children were apart for a long time and the active military person was in the combat zone," she says, "so with that in mind, we gave them a little extra leeway when they got pushy. There were always complaints about not having a choice of meals or not being able to get soda or beer. Many of them did not understand that service on a military charter flight was different from a commercial airline. The government mandated what we could and could not serve. The children were often snotty brats, something that seemed odd when you'd think a military family would be well disciplined.

We were so used to the lovely young boys. All I can say is that when the dependents reached their final destination, we were glad to see them go."

Chapter 4
Destination: Vietnam

Commercial jets that carried troops to and from Vietnam had about a thousand square feet within its cabins, cockpits and cargo areas. But it is impossible to measure or count the number of stories and memories from inside those planes.

Unlike today, where depending on their seniority, flight attendants pick a schedule of what days they want to work and where they want to fly, during the Vietnam War there was no bidding to get certain trips. Flight attendants were told what to do and the only thing that was certain about the trip was the stops along the way. Patti Medaris (Culea) flew with Flying Tiger Line based in Oakland, California.

"We usually began our workday in the afternoon," she said, "with a 45-minute bus ride from Oakland north to Travis Air Force Base just east of Fairfield. Troops, usually Army, would be at the base in uniform and ready to go."

Flying Tiger Line crew

* * * * *

World Airways flight attendant Helen Tennant (Hegelheimer) says it was important for the five flight attendants on a Boeing 707 to quickly establish control over the 165 military troops on board.

On May 26, 2014, she spoke at the Women's Vietnam Memorial.

Helen Tennant (Hegelheimer) 2014

"One of the things we did was play a lot of games with Army versus Navy versus Marine Corps. During our training we were trained on all ranks, patches and insignias. We knew them very well. I recall the First Marine Division coming on the airplane with a lot of bravado on our way to Vietnam."

"First of all we called them *Army* and they would let us know that, no, they were Marines. So then we would say 'you must be the 101st Airborne Division.'"

"Quickly, we let them know we knew they were jarheads and they were with the First Marine Division and they should sit down and fasten their seat belt or else this was going to be a very long flight.

"We did that conversely with the Army, too," she says. "The first Cavalry Division has a horse on their patch."

"We gave them a ration about their *storied past*, which we all knew the history of. It was always fun to see Army Screaming Eagles and Airborne come on board and we called them the First Marine Division."

* * * * *

Patti Medaris (Culea) remembers flying from Oakland to either San Bernardino or El Toro Marine Base in Santa Ana to pick up a planeload of Marines. There was always a routine.

"A sergeant was in charge and had the men file up the ladder," she says. "Each Marine carried a rifle and as they came on board they handed their ammunition clips to us and we put them in a canvas bag. Of course there was no assigned seating, they loaded back to front, three seats on the right and three on the left with an aisle up the middle."

*****

"From Travis," Patti said, "our plane would be in the air about five hours, traveling 2,500 miles to Anchorage, Alaska.

"We usually landed at the main airport in Anchorage but other airlines would use Elmendorf Air Force Base about eleven miles north."

World Airways MD-11 loading troops at Elmendorf AFB, Alaska

"Once in Anchorage, we would stay overnight at the Hotel Captain Cook."

"But for the troops, their journey had a long way to go. The soldiers or Marines would get off the plane at Anchorage and head to a bar to stretch their legs and have several rounds of drinks. While that was going on the plane would be refueled and another crew would come on board to prepare for the flight to Okinawa. The troops had about an hour on the ground and then after boarding, the plane would lift off for the flight across the Pacific."

For Patti and her crewmates, they would meet a new group of young men in the next day or two. She said, "The next morning, we would relieve a crew that had come in that day with another load of troops. We then flew 4,400 miles in ten and a half hours to Okinawa."

Photo: Al Simms, Radar Section, 1st 14th Arty

"Once there, our flight crew would head to a nearby hotel but the troops still had the last leg of their journey to make. They were given another hour break in Okinawa to get off the plane and stretch their legs and bend their elbows at a nearby bar before being told to get back on board."

When the young men took their seats, Patti said they had new faces to look at. "The troops would be greeted by a relief flight crew who would then fly them to South Vietnam into one of three airfields: Da Nang to the north, Saigon in the middle or Cam Ranh Bay south of Da Nang on the coast." Patti shook her head, remembering when she was on a crew for the final leg and recalled the exhausted looks on the young men's faces. "From the time their flight took off from Travis to when they walked down the stairs and their feet touched the ground in Vietnam could take the better part of 24 hours."

* * * * *

This is not to say the flight attendants were immune to exhaustion. Patti remembers what happened on one trip to Vietnam that was extended over several days because other crewmembers were ill.

"I was wiped out so much that I fell asleep on a soldier's shoulder and drooled. I was so embarrassed but he loved it and said he wasn't going to wash his uniform."

Patti and her Flying Tiger colleagues flew the northern route, but there were other ways of getting to the combat zone. Pan Am's flight out of Oakland sometimes went to Hawaii. All troops left the plane to hang out in the terminal while the plane was refueled, and a new flight crew took over. Unlike Alaska, troops were not allowed outside the terminal in Hawaii but had only glimpses of the tropical paradise.

The second stop of the journey after Hawaii was Guam at a military airport with not much of a terminal. The troops had to be back in the air in 45 minutes bound for the Philippine Islands.

Once in the Philippines, troops were allowed to wander through the terminal and go outside to look around. The plane always parked at least 200 yards from the terminal meaning troops were often soaked by frequent rain showers and were soaked by the time they reached shelter.

The terminal concourse was jammed with hawkers selling everything from electronics to watches, clothing, food, beer, and hand-made products and inside the bathrooms, drugs.

Fredene Weaver (Maulhardt) of World Airways remembers how the mood of soldiers changed once out of the Philippines. "When we were back in the air, it seems the soldiers mood became more somber as they got closer to Vietnam. It might have been the effects of beer or marijuana but many of them were clearly thinking about what they were about to face."

For Leslie Laird (Pfeifer), her first flight assignment brought an indelible memory as she watched young faces that would soon turn old slowly climb on board. There was fear in some eyes, a deadpan stare in others. And for all flight attendants who were on these flights, they wondered how many boys would not come back alive.

* * * * *

Janet Bancroft (Burttram) made this observation: "The Boeing 707 military configuration was 165 passengers. We were told that 165 soldiers died every day."

And for Patti Medaris (Culea), "Knowing we would lose 10% of every plane load we brought in broke our hearts.

"We'd walk the aisle at night and see these young men trying to be brave. I remember seeing one soldier sucking his thumb. How our hearts ached for them, and yes, we kissed them. I don't know of any of the Tiger girls ever going into the heads with the boys, but maybe they did. I was such an innocent then. We did sit on their laps, played cards with them, exchanged addresses, wrote them and encouraged them as much as we could. They were always taking our pictures. We felt like movie stars."

For Nancy Wood (Shamel), a World Airways flight attendant from May 1967 to June 1969 the flights to Vietnam were awful. "The guys were young and scared, they didn't want to talk to anyone," she said.

Jeannie Wagers (Wiseman) tried to keep things loose, especially when giving pre-flight instructions.

"I would say something like, 'A complete set of instructions are located in the seat pocket and for the Army, we have pictures'."

* * * * *

The reality that young men were headed to the killing fields and jungles of Vietnam made flying troops between Point U.S.A. and Point V even more difficult because part of the flight attendant's job was to lift the spirits of those on board. Unlike today, there were no in-flight movies for the troops to watch.

Continental's Dottie Hawker, Jeannie Hopkins and Debby Smith

World Airway's Janet Bancroft (Burttram)

There were usually card games and sometimes flight attendants would join in.

1967 Courtesy Pan Am

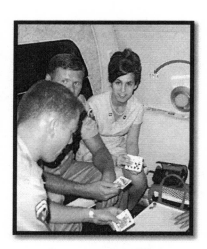

Courtesy BJ Elliott
Behind My Wings

Janet Bancroft (Burttram) remembers impromptu entertainment.

"One of my early purchases was a Hashimoto, six string gut guitar. In fact, I brought it on the military trips because there were so many musically talented soldiers. Their eyes would light up and take turns playing for us and played their hearts out. They even used the PA mike at times. I still have the guitar but it's covered in a mound of dust. They used us as confessors. We were their moms, sisters, wives and girlfriends. They would pour out their emotions. It was important to listen."

But while listening, most flight attendants knew to expect a standard line from a soldier or Marine who was trying to get a kiss. Said World Airways Fredene Weaver (Maulhardt), "I lost track of the number of times I heard, 'This may be my last day to kiss a girl.'"

One of the few who did not hear that line was World Airways flight attendant Jeannine Wagers (Wiseman). But she does remember the one time she was kissed on an airplane.

Jeannie Wagers (Wiseman)

"The only guy who ever touched me was a New Zealander and he was in the first row. Just before we landed he said something to me, and I said, 'pardon?' and he grabbed me and gave me a lip smack and kiss and then turned around and said, 'and I did that with me seat belt fastened!'"

* * * * *

Continental Airlines flight attendant Bea Weber remembers one special Halloween when they were taking soldiers to Vietnam.

"The first leg was to Okinawa and we had a stop in Honolulu," she said. "The troops got off the plane and while we were refueling, we flight attendants used the time to buy a few things and decorate the plane. When the guys came back, we had a Halloween party."

Bea Weber with the troops on Halloween 1968

* * * * *

On another flight, Bea and her flight attendants brought a life-size reminder of home to Marines in Da Nang.

With a chuckle in her voice she said, "On our way to Vietnam during a stopover in Honolulu at a drug store we spotted a larger-than-life-size cardboard cut-out of a blonde in a swim suit that was part of an ad for sun tan oil. We asked the store manager if we could take it for the troops in Vietnam."

They got permission and hauled the card board model they called 'Sally' on the plane. Once she arrived in Da Nang, Marines probably rubbed their eyes in disbelief when "Sally" reported for morale-building duty.

"Sally" with Marines in Da Nang

* * * * *

On social media today are memories of being on board other planes. Some come from author John Podalski whose work includes the compelling book *Cherries: A Vietnam War Novel*.

Courtesy: John Podalski

John writes on Facebook about leaving for Vietnam in 1970:
"I was one of 200 teenage soldiers aboard a Pan American Boeing 707 jet airliner.

John Podalski
Courtesy: John Podalski

"We were packed inside, not an empty seat to be had . . .the flight felt more like the beginning of a great adventure to most of us. Not a soul slept on the plane for fear of missing out on something. . . only a few remained seated.

"Small groups huddled together across the length of the plane – some of those seated were surrounded by soldiers who knelt on seats and stood in the aisles. Each group was comprised of young men who knew one another from earlier military training; they had much in common and spent much of their time commiserating about their experiences during the last six months.

"Most of the African American soldiers migrated to the rear of the aircraft. There were several small groups, many of them strangers and meeting for the first time, but it didn't take long for them to warm up to one another. Like the other groups throughout the cabin, discussions were about anything and everything; bouts of spontaneous laughter erupted sporadically from around the cabin. After a couple of hours into the flight, those soldiers in the rear of the plane broke out in song and began a singing competition. Each group got a chance to perform, but had to sing Motown songs made famous by the Four Tops, Temptations, Smokey Robinson and the Miracles, Marvin Gaye and others. And truth be told, every group was very good – earning applause from many of the passengers after each song. Unfortunately, this was our only entertainment, but it was great while it lasted.

"I remember many of those discussions on the flight. Most were about girlfriends or wives left behind – of course, everyone had pictures to pass around. Others talked about special events in their life, muscle cars, sports championships, drinking, and of course, their fear of going to war.

"Stewardesses were seen more so than not and seemed to travel along the aisles nonstop during our flight."

Pan Am flight attendant Maureen Van Leeuwen on a Boeing 707, 1968

"Dressed in their Pan American flight uniforms and mini-skirts, their passing usually resulted in cat calls, whistles, or proposals of marriage. Every passenger in an aisle seat leaned over into the narrow aisle to watch the lovely ladies sashay up the aisle – admiring their legs and hoping to catch a glimpse of something more. The view was only good for a couple rows before bobbing heads in front of you blocked the view. This also proved to be dangerous; many passengers butted heads in the aisle in their haste to move into position. These collisions resulted in nothing more than dancing stars and a large, sore bump on the noggin. Many firmly believed the stewardesses were doing this purposely to see our reactions."

John Podalski today
Courtesy: John Podalski

Navy Lieutenant Richard Scharff was a 28-year-old Reserve Supply Officer pressed into duty and sent to the Naval Support Activity in Da Nang.

In 2019, Scharff, then 80 during an interview in Coronado, California recalled with the author his memories of his first trip to Vietnam. He was on board a Continental 707 with about ten other officers and the remainder of the plane that seated 175 was packed with enlisted Marines.

Lt. Richard Scharff 1966 and Dick Scharff 2019

"It was a raucous group with six flight attendants on board," he said. "The troops were singing songs and having a great time," he said. Then his expression changed. "They didn't know what the hell they were getting into but they had a great time going over."

For Dick Scharff, the reality of what he got himself into hit home when on January 31, 1968, the first night of the Tet Offensive, a person he got to know while in SERE (Survival, Evasion, Resistance and Escape) training near San Diego, LTJG Robert Moinester was killed. While defending a ramp at Hue, the unit under Moinester's command came under hostile mortar fire and Moinester organized his men into an infantry platoon of Navy, Marine Corps and Army personnel and went house-to-house in a clearing operation. The enemy was driven from their positions and took heavy casualties but Moinester was killed in the firefight.

LTJG Robert Moinester   USS Moinester (FF-1097)
1943-1968

Moinester was awarded the Silver Star (Posthumously) for his valor and
the USS Moinester a Knox-class frigate is named for him.

* * * * *

Flight attendant Janet Bancroft (Burttram) recalls her first trip with
World Airways, a two-week assignment from the U.S. to Sydney, Australia.
   "Normally we went from a U.S. base to Yokota, Japan (crew rest),
Yokota to Saigon to Darwin, Australia (crew rest) Darwin, Sydney, Darwin
(crew rest) and either turn around to Vietnam or turn around to Sydney from
Darwin for the rest of the trip. That's why we were gone so long. We always
stayed in Darwin.

   "On my first trip they were repairing the runway in Darwin, so we
couldn't land there. Therefore, after we left Yokota we flew to Saigon and
overnighted there. Stayed at the Majestic Hotel and experienced mortar fire
rounds across the river (Mekong Delta)."

Hotel Majestic, Saigon

"It shook the hotel and was a little unnerving. The hotel was an old French hotel, very tropical with a caged elevator. When you were in the elevator you could see out as you passed through the floors."

Hotel Majestic lobby

"We had a curfew and were restricted to two blocks, with a guard. There was a bar we all went to which was packed with G.I's. I can remember telling them about our hotel and the 'foot bath' in the bathrooms. Naive me. That was when I learned what a 'bidet' was. I was so embarrassed! I had a lot to learn about this world. But, that's why I wanted to travel, to learn. It was VERY unusual for the crew and plane to stay in the war zone."

* * * * *

"As an all-female cabin crew (three of us)," Janet remembers, "we were encouraged to visit the Saigon USO which wasn't too far from the hotel. We were given free burgers and got to meet the G.I.'s. A year or so later when I was 'leased' to Air Vietnam with two other flight attendants we met three really great guys at the USO who were in town on a mission. From there we went to a local nightclub that had a band from the Philippines that were very good impersonating just about any group. However, we didn't stay long because the 'bar girls' there didn't appreciate American girls invading their territory."

Janet Bancroft (Burttram)

"So, the fellows we were with offered to take us to their base and soon we were off in their jeep (told no one) up route 5 (I think) and went past a large U.S. field hospital to a little camp called Cu Chi."

On the road to Cu Chi

"Well, I have since learned this is where the 'tunnel rats' were!"

Australian soldier kneeling over an open trap door

Part of a tunnel at Cu Chi made wider and taller for tourists

"Viet Cong lived in the ground and went from place to place via the tunnels they dug. We saw refugee camps along the way of civilians who had no homes.

"What struck me were the number of families of many Army of Republic of Vietnam soldiers who had their families living with them in lean-to shelters and using outdoor cooking set-ups near where they would leave to go fight the enemy. In some ways the ARVN soldiers had an advantage over our soldiers who were thousands of miles from home and family.

"We got back to Saigon too late for the G.I's to return to their base because they had a darkness curfew. So they had to stay with us at the Caravelle Hotel."

Caravelle Hotel, Saigon

"That was interesting. I still remember the name of one of the guys because he went to the same military college (Norwich University in Northfield, Vermont) my Dad went to."

The guy she remembered was Tom Luczynski, then a 24-year-old Army infantry captain and advisor to the Vietnamese 33rd Ranger Battalion.

Captain Thomas Luczynski
1971

Captain Luczynski worked with a 250-member battalion about 30 miles north of Saigon and along with four of his men would come into Saigon once a week for a shower, change of clothes and a visit to the Caravelle Hotel for a beer.

(Author's note: While researching the book, former flight attendant Janet

Bancroft (Burttram) shared her story of meeting the Army men in 1971 at the Caravelle Hotel. Janet tried multiple times to reach Tom, the one she thought was at the hotel and traveled with to Cu Chi and in late January 2019 she finally made contact and received an E-mail back. This was some of the reply:

January 22, 2019
Janet:
What a pleasant surprise to receive your email. I think that was 47 years ago, (give or take). A lot of water has gone over the dam in all those years. I still have vivid memories of my experience in Vietnam, but nothing tragic. Fortunately for me, I made it back in one piece, and a year after I returned my brother followed in my footsteps and did the same. He was also a Norwich graduate - Class of '69, mine was Class of '68. . . . .to say the least, it was refreshing to talk with you then, because mostly I only talked with Vietnamese. In fact, I frequently went days without even talking to an American, even my own team.
Thanks again for contacting me.
Fondest regards,
Tom

* * * * *

Luczynski, in a telephone call with the author from Ohio, reflected on the infrequent contact he had with Americans while in Vietnam.

"We were vagabonds on patrol," he said, "and sometimes went 17 straight days in the jungle and only saw an American once every three days when they re-supplied us from helicopters."

Luczynski remembers not talking with anyone except Vietnamese. "Talking with an American was great. I would go up to a helicopter pilot and say, 'Hey, say something to me,' and I'd shake their hand and they'd look at me kind of strange."

"The pilot would reply, 'What do you want me to say?'"

Answering back Luczynski would tell the man, "I just want to hear some English."

* * * * *

Luczynski's encounter with Janet was the only time he saw her, which is why he was so surprised to receive a letter from her.

"Who would ever remember me from 47 years ago?" he asks.

Captain Thomas Lucyznski   Thomas Luczynski 2019
receiving Biet Don Quan
(Vietnamese Ranger Badge)
1970

Luczynski believes flight attendants then were able to make more of a lasting first impression than today.

Saturn Airlines flight attendants

"Nobody made it through airline stewardess school unless they were very attractive," he says. "They didn't have to be beauty queens, but they kept themselves well; underweight or at least no overweight. Now it's a totally different scenario. You don't know what you're going to get."

Luczynski flew to Vietnam on Flying Tiger Line and the same airline brought him back home, the only time he traveled on civilian military charters during his time in the combat zone.

* * * * *

Former World Airways flight attendant Lorna McLearie has a connection with the old Caravelle Hotel.

Lorna McLearie

"The month I was there the USO building was bombed. We had moved from the Caravelle Hotel to a newly built hotel named the Palace, which was not fully finished with construction. I remember climbing stairs to the roof one day to be in the sun and escape the noise."

She also has memories of the Continental Hotel in Saigon.

Continental Hotel 1968

"One day at the Continental Hotel in Saigon (where Hemingway once hung out and wrote there in 1937) while I was there it was filled with journalists from around the world. I noticed French architecture surrounded in barbwire outside of the open-air restaurant. An overwhelming sadness swept over me. So much destruction and I was in a safe zone, but we had curfews and at times slept in a cot at the airport during the night. Certain hours of travel were not safe from hotel to airport."

Pranks, Games and a Smoke-filled Plane

Fredene Weaver (Maulhardt) remembers with fondness the pilots she flew with and for the most part, said all of the crews treated the flight attendants with respect.

Patti Medaris (Culea) agreed. "Most of the pilots were like 'dads' to me. Maybe it was because I was small, but I only had one pilot who bothered me."

It involved a pilot who crossed the line when it came to practical jokes and it happened on only her second or third flight with Flying Tigers in late 1967 from Travis Air Force Base to Anchorage, Alaska.

While she cannot remember the pilot's name, Patti has no problem recalling other things about him.

"He was a good-looking guy," she said. "I heard other girls tell me he thought he was God's gift to women. He was in love with himself and they said he looked for every chance to embarrass the girls on the plane."

One of Patti's duties was to instruct the troops on board the 707 how to use oxygen masks that dropped in front of each passenger during an emergency.

"The pilot knew I was the newest person on the flight," Patti remembered. "And as I was about to demonstrate how to use the oxygen mask, when I went to put it over my nose and mouth, a Kotex tampon pad fell out. All of the soldiers near me began laughing. I was mortified and the other girls on the plane got really upset because we knew who had put it there." (Note: the airline regularly had tampon pads in the plane's lavatories.)

Patti composed herself as best as she could and thought to herself, "That's OK. I'll get back at him."

At the time, Patti was taking medication for a bladder infection and the pills had a side effect of turning her urine blue.

"When the pilots called and said they wanted coffee," she said, "I put one of my pills in the captain's cup."

Patti raises her eyebrows when she remembers what soon happened. "They had an ambulance waiting on the runway in Anchorage to take the pilot away who had no idea why his pee was blue."

Today she realizes the harm she could have caused, but at the time it seemed like a good idea.

"It was not the smartest thing to do. I guess when they got him to the hospital they ran some tests and knew what had happened. Thankfully, he was not hurt."

Patti never saw "God's gift" again. He did not continue on the flight and she thinks he returned home.

* * * * *

Janet Bancroft (Burttram) remembers another part of the pre-flight demonstrations that was uncomfortable.

"We had a senior flight attendant nick-named 'Reno' Rose. She was from Reno, and her name was Rose. She had a great personality and introduced the cabin crew to the passengers. She called us Miss *Chevious*, Miss *Taken*, Miss *Understood* and Miss *Handled* by the Captain. That always got a chuckle.

"There were no dividers between cabins. It was one long plane. Imagine donning a life vest during the demo with 165 pairs of eyes on you while you are blowing into the tubes of the vest. Always made me blush."

* * * * *

Jeannie Wagers (Wiseman) remembers a pilot who kidded her about her age.

"He tried to put me down by saying I was older than he was. So, I turned to him and said, 'Well, that's alright, Captain, I have more hair than you've got.'"

* * * * *

A not-so clear and present danger for flight attendants on MAC flights during the Vietnam War was the constant presence of second-hand cigarette smoke. It was not until July 1977 that Aurigny Air Services became the first airline to ban smoking entirely on its flights. By 2000 smoking was prohibited on all domestic and international flights.

But during the Vietnam War, cigarettes were cheap and smoking was a way of life for military personnel and for a soldier or Marine on their way to Vietnam, a greater health concern was if they could stay out of the way of a bullet or a land mine.

"The cigarette smoke was awful," Patti Medaris (Culea) remembers. "But it was for the boys and how could they be denied that?"

For Patti it was a case of "when in a smoke-filled cabin do what the smokers do."

"When we weren't needed in the cabin, some of us girls would go up in the cockpit one at a time and smoke Crooks cigars with the pilots. The cigars were soaked in rum and we loved them."

Patti also remembers playing what was called "wheel roulette." "The spokes on the nose wheel were marked," she said, "and we'd put money on a number and whichever spoke was straight down when the blocks were put on was the winner. I won a couple of times."

Pot Shots and Mechanicals

Every plane coming into Vietnam was a moving target. Flight attendant Leslie Laird (Pfeifer) made more than 70 trips to Vietnam for Flying Tiger Line, usually landing in Da Nang that was near the demilitarized zone. "Our planes took pot shots from civilians in the rice paddies we flew over. Usually this was on approach when we were lower to the ground. After landing, flight engineers would do a walk around the plane to check damage. You could see the little pings on the skin of the aircraft."

Leslie says she and the crew never were on the ground for more than a couple of hours. "We couldn't stay there because it was too dangerous," she said. "When we landed during red alerts, the returning soldiers would muster on the airstrip to board. There were bullet holes in the belly of our aircraft."

* * * * *

Airlift International's Gretchen Bergstresser (Garren) recalled a harrowing moment when the 727 she was on landed at Da Nang airport on a flight from Okinawa.

"We landed in Da Nang, the cockpit crew was in ops, and were just hanging out in the airplane when soldiers came running down the aisle screaming to get off the airplane, saying we were under attack. We were sitting in the front of the airplane and we boarded the passengers through the aft stairs. We all jumped up and ran through the plane and down the stairs to the ramp. We were in the middle of mass chaos of sirens blaring and people running for cover in every direction. The soldiers told us to run and pointed to a bunker across the ramp. Knowing this was for real we all started running, and one of the girls fell and another one lost a shoe, and someone grabbed the girl who fell and flung her over his shoulder and ran past us. The next thing I know I have a guy on each side of me lifting my feet off the ground and running into the bunker. We were all safe and sound, and we got the all clear that it was okay to board the plane again. What a thriller: we looked a mess. One girl had skinned knees, another lost the heel to her shoe, and we all were pretty rattled, but a plane full of Marines made up for that!"

* * * * *

Flight attendants were always on alert for potential danger while in the war zone. Former Flying Tiger flight attendant Marsha Hay (Merz) remembers a moment during her first year of flying in 1969 and to this day wonders if she averted a potential tragedy.

Marsha Hay (Merz) 1970

(In the above photo the author was not sure what was written on the sash. Thinking it might be part of a beauty pageant, I asked Marsha and she said the words were REMOVE BEFORE FLIGHT. The sash was attached to a metal gear pin that was put into the nose gear to prevent someone in the cockpit from inadvertently pulling up the nose gear while the plane was on the ground. She decided it would make a nice photo and it did.)

Now here is Marsha's story:

"I was on a flight from Yokota AFB, Japan to Da Nang. We were late and the sun was going down when we landed. Once in Da Nang, our passengers disembarked down the ramps, the Vietnamese cleaners came onboard and went to work while we were refueling (for the flight back to Yokota). An hour or two later it was dark and the senior flight attendant announced that passenger boarding was starting at the forward main cabin door. Since I was in the back of the plane near the aft left galley, I watched as the cleaning people hurried out of the airplane and down the aft ramp. Just then I noticed a large plastic bag full of what I thought were trash or cleaning supplies. I picked up the plastic bag and was going to put it on the ramp, but the big white ramp was already moving back from the aircraft. The ramp was driven by a G.I. I yelled to the cleaners and ramp man, 'You forgot this bag and I have no room for it.' They looked up at me and then apparently noticed something else under the aircraft fuselage. They pointed to something attached to fuselage below where I was standing. When they did that, one of the cleaners quickly started walking away. The guy driving the ramp said, 'It looks like a satchel charge, you need to empty the plane.' Unfortunately, we had just started boarding passengers from the forward main cabin door. I called the senior flight attendant and told her about the satchel charge and my assessment that it could be a bomb attached to the fuselage under the aft main cabin door. Immediately, everyone was ordered out the forward main cabin door and the passengers and crew were ushered away from the aircraft while a military team removed something. A G.I. explained to me that a satchel charge was a bomb in a bag with a timer used to detonate it. We then re-boarded the aircraft and took off. I'm sorry to say I was never told what was removed and have always wondered if it really was a bomb."

Marsha Hay (Merz) at FTLPA Reunion May 2019
* * * * *
When you have a 300,000-pound flying machine there are bound to be

moments when things don't always work perfectly. A catch-all phrase used when a plane is delayed for a variety of reasons is "mechanicals."

Explaining the delay to passengers takes diplomacy, good judgment and sometimes a sense of humor.

World Airways flight attendant Jeannie Wagers (Wiseman) recalls a time when the plane she was on had some backfiring *booms* as it began moving on the tarmac. The noise came from compressor stalls, but she noticed some passengers had a look of concern.

"Couldn't have that," she says today, "comfort and cared-for only. So, I picked up the PA microphone and said, 'Our aircraft appears to have gas on its tummy, and we are going back to the gate to burp it.' Seemed to take care of attitude concerns."

Chapter 5
The Letters

Heart-wrenching loneliness and isolation for young men sent to jungles a half world away were constant reminders of what they left behind.

In the middle of stifling heat, monsoon rain, mosquitos, dysentery, mud, jungle bugs, firefights and body bags, thoughts often turned to the sweet faces and smiles of the last American woman they had seen.

Vivid memories were recalled of young women who had walked up and down the aisles of planes that brought the troops to war. Some men after coaxing a name out of a flight attendant scrawled it on a piece of paper. Then in tents, mess halls or on patrol, emotions were put in letters that were mailed to those women. Exact addresses were not needed, only the flight attendant's name and her airline. No postage was required, just the word "Free" in the envelope's upper right hand corner if mailed from the combat zone.

When flight attendants returned to their bases, their mailboxes would be jammed with letters from the troops who had been on their flights.

In his book, "The Vietnam War in Popular Culture," Ron Milam wrote about World Airways flight attendant Helen Tennant (Hegelheimer).

"In 1966 and 1967 she flew on hundreds of troop transport flights in and out of the United States, Japan, and Vietnam, including Da Nang, Ton Son Nhut/Saigon, and Bien Hoa.

She exchanged names and addresses with many soldiers she met on the flights. Soon she had a pile of letters with names and faces she could not remember. To solve that, Helen and her fellow flight attendants came up with an idea.

"This is 1966, 1967," she said. "We would go down to the local liquor store and buy up all of the *Playboy* magazines. Number one, women didn't do that in 1966, number two it made the liquor store manager mad, but we did it anyhow, and we had a mass mailing and every address that we had we would send that troop a *Playboy* magazine and we would get letters back saying how popular they were--a *stewardess* sent them a *Playboy* magazine so it made their day."

* * * * *

In 2004, Helen's experiences of 1966-1967 appeared on the online forum popasmoke.com.

"Going over, there were usually two legs---Travis Air Force Base to Japan and Japan to Vietnam. From California the troops did a lot of letter writing. Guys would ask me, 'Is this a good letter? If you received this, would you wait for me?' At first I read the letters, but they really pulled at your heart, so after a while I would just pretend to read them and say they were perfect. There were always some chatty guys who wanted to talk and if we had any special unit guys----Green Berets or Airborne Rangers---there was a lot of bravado. They spoke proudly of their training; how difficult it was for them not to get 'washed out'. Over time I realized they weren't trying to impress me as much as they were trying to convince themselves their training would help them."

Janet Bancroft (Burttram) also heard the bravado.

"On some flights there were a few with some bravado who had 're-upped' for the third or fourth time. They didn't mind going back to Vietnam and they were paid $1000 or something to 're-up.' I always thought they were a little over the top."

Helen Tennant (Hegelheimer) continues:

"These were boys destined for combat and they had been told in training what their expected mortality rate was. But most of the guys were pretty quiet. They asked us for alcohol and we said, 'If the military wanted you to have that they would have put it in the contract.'

"When we got to Yokota Air Force Base in Japan we had a crew change. So after a layover, I'd get on another plane with a group of guys I hadn't met who had already been on the plane for 12 hours. We had to kind of feel out the mood. By then they were usually very quiet. It was five hours to Vietnam and five hours back. We called this the Vietnam turnaround. We'd go in and out with minimal ground time. It was the senior stew's position to be at the top of the ramp when the men got off in Vietnam, but nobody wanted that job, nothing disparaging to the other gals, but some just couldn't do it. I never said 'good-bye' or 'good luck'. I would shake their hand, look them in the eye, smile, and say 'See you later'. Sometimes I'd say 'See you in 12 months'. They really wanted somebody to look at them. At the top of the ramp was the world; at the bottom of the ramp was the war. At that moment, at the top of the ramp, I was their wife, their sister, their girlfriend, and for those troops who had no one else—and there were many—I was their mother."

Helen's memories were similar to those of World Airways flight attendant Janet Bancroft (Burttram) who flew with the airline two years after Helen left.

"I'll never forget one guy," Janet says, "who looked like someone's kid brother, come up to me at the bottom of the stairs on embarking for R & R to Sydney. He was so tongue-tied because he hadn't seen a girl in 11 months. He simply was shy and bashful but needed to express his awe at seeing us. And those are the ones who talked; you wondered what was going on in the minds of the ones who didn't."

Helen Tennant (Hegelheimer) continues her thoughts about caring personally for the wellbeing of troops on her flights.

"That was the most important thing I've ever done. I don't think there was one of us who did not want to keep them on the plane. That's why some of the girls were back in the bathrooms crying. We were very aware that we were sending them to war and that some would never come back. Therein lies the guilt. We never showed any emotion in front of the troops but we sure drank a lot when we got back to Japan. We substituted booze for crying.

"The first thing we'd ask when we arrived in Vietnam is, 'Are we taking troops out?' If you took 165 men in and 165 men out, you really could fool yourself into believing they were all coming home. But in '66 and '67 the war was escalating so we often left Vietnam with an empty plane. There was nothing else to say other than, 'They're not all coming home.' It would just slam you right in the face. And when we got back to Japan we drank even heavier."

* * * * *

Patti Medaris (Culea) received many letters from the young men who were on her flights and still has several today. She and other Flying Tiger flight attendants would reply to some letters but others such as two that follow were too personal and were best left unanswered.

The letters came from Tony (last name withheld), a Marine who had flown with Patti just once. The first was written on November 18, 1967.

Tony told Patti about a fight he had with another Marine that resulted in his court martial and a demotion of two ranks. It seems the other Marine was telling everyone that Patti had long dark red underpants.

long ones and I almost killed him so I lost two stripes I was a cpl. and now I'm a P.F.C. so I tolded him you don't talk like that about my girlfriend so I hit him with my fist and I broke his jaw. So Patti I want you

to really be my girl so when I get back to Frisco I could marrie you if you let me.

He asked Patti for a photo of herself and other flight attendants and promised to send her a picture of himself as soon as he could find someone who had a camera. His closing line shows how vulnerable young hearts could be.

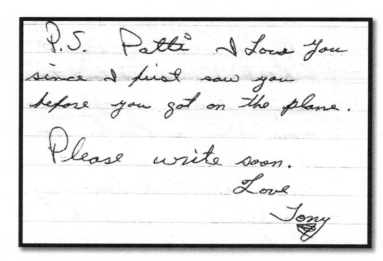

P.S. Patti I Love You since I first saw you before you got on the plane.

Please write soon.
Love
Tony

Tony wrote a second letter on November 22, 1967.

My Darling Patti,

He again asked for a picture of Patti and then wrote about his wish to marry her.

if you could wait until July 11, 1970 because that is the date I get out but if you want to marrie me right after I come back from Viet Nam and you might want me to stay in the Marine Corps

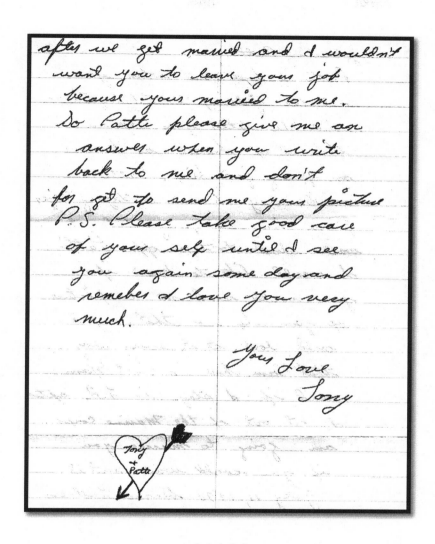

* * * * *

A letter from another Marine was from Bruce (last name withheld), a
Private First Class. He wrote to Patti January 18, 1968 and she answered this
one.

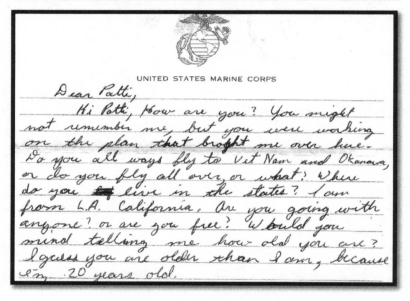

Bruce wrote about being on Patti's flight on December 20, 1967.

I guess I might say when your Plane flow me here, that was on the 20th of Dec. Now you might remember me, but you see so many guys that you can't remember all the guys.
Will I have to go for now, but before I do, I will give you my adress, so if you have a littly time you might wright back.

Love
Bruce

You never know, but the flight could have been one into Da Nang that Patti documented showing a visit from Santa on the tarmac. Santa was actually a flight attendant dressed in a Santa costume with borrowed GI boots to complete the outfit.

"We always had a Santa on every flight on Christmas time," she says.

Da Nang Christmas 1967

In the letter, Bruce mentioned a girl back home who he was engaged to and added:

> *you and her have something in common and that is you names and your both very ~~[crossed out]~~ buttyful and if you do wright back would you please send me a picture of you?*

The letter was general enough that Patti sent a reply to the 20-year-old Marine wishing him the best and thanking him for his kind words.

* * * * *

When the author was in television news, one of the stories in the 1980's involved a trip to Washington, D.C. and a visit to the Vietnam Wall where the names of those killed during the war are etched in black granite.

Patti wanted me to look up the names of the young men who wrote to her.

John, at the Vietnam Wall in Washington, D.C.

Tragically, Tony and Bruce, the two 20-year-old Marines mentioned above, were killed in action. Tony died on January 24, 1968 in Quang Tri Province near the district capital Khe Sanh, two months after writing to Patti.

Bruce was killed in Quang Nam not far from Da Nang, site of heavy fighting during the war due to its close distance to communist North Vietnam. He was with the First Marine Division and died during a firefight on May 16, 1968, four months and two days after writing his letter to the pretty flight attendant.

More Letters

A common concern for GI's who wrote letters to flight attendants was that the young ladies might not remember them. Typical was this letter from Scott (last name withheld):

"Hello Patti,
How's my favorite "flying Tiger" I trust the world is treating you alright.

"We were on a flight together from Travis to Anchorage. You were my most accommodating stewardess and I portrayed the roll of being your most obnoxious passenger.
Remember, I remarked that we were sort of like neighbors because I lived in Newport Beach on the peninsula and you just lived down a piece. I asked you if you would like to correspond with a Marine stationed in Vietnam. I was seated in the rear section of the aircraft on the port side in a middle seat. In fact, you also surrendered your address to the guy sitting next to me in the aisle seat. His name was Dave. Still no help sweetheart, well I was the one with two wedding rings on my left hand, you know, the tall dark, handsome one (Smile!).
I don't think you're in the habit of giving out your address at request, so actually it shouldn't be too difficult for you to determine who I am.

Hoping to hear from you soon!
Scott

(Patti answered Scott's letter)

This was from Donnie Ray (last name withheld):

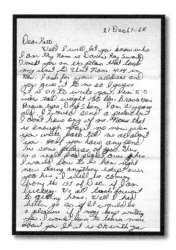

Dec 21, 1967
This is a real bad place over here. I would love to be home right now, doing anything except over here. I will be coming home the 1st of December if I am lucky. We all look forward to getting home. Please write. If not, just say so and I won't bother you. I would rather be there and give you a big kiss for Christmas. Well, be sweet.
Love always,
Donnie Ray

(Patti answered Donnie Ray's letter)

Then came a letter from Rick (last name withheld).

Hi Pattie,
How is my favorite stewardess on the Flying Tiger Airlines?
Sure do wish I had more time to get to know you a little better but I guess

that's the breaks.
I know you probably won't answer this letter. But you can't blame me for trying can you?
Hoping for an answer
P.F.C. Rick

Patti eventually answered but before Rick received her reply, he wrote again.

"It gets so darn lonely when you are out in the field that you have to write. If you don't you go about nuts. I sure hope you don't mind me writing to you. I'm not much at writing but you will have to take in consideration that I am just a GI. I guess I had better close for now. Charlie is starting to fire a few rounds at us.
Hoping for answers,
PFC Rick

A PFC named Paul (last name withheld) wrote to Patti, thanking her for writing back to him.

"Feb 23, 1968
From Lon Binh, South Vietnam
Temp-90's Low 60's
Dear Patti,
Yes, it was nice hearing from you, you've got good writing and sound like a nice person. I bet your fun to be with, take out also, I forgot how old are you how many bros and sisters you got?
Where is Hermosa Beach located at? Boy! that's what I am looking for in a house-wife that can cook, sew, iron and etc. love to go out and have fun, and sports of all kinds, that's what I want to do after I get out of services, get married, got 11 months to go.
I'll say one thing you was a cute girl, have you got a picture.
Been in services a year-20 Feb. 68, Time and the days sure fly over here?"

Paul used stationery that included a map at the bottom of Southeast Asia with a line pointing to Saigon and a note "23 miles from there."

Paul told Patti he was from Quincy, Illinois and hoped to be promoted to Specialist 4th Class soon and said he would take his R & R either in Bangkok or Sydney and asked which is best.

He signed the letter "Love, Paul."

* * * * *

There were common threads that ran through letters to flight attendants. Loneliness and anticipation of coming home but there was also uncertainty whether or not the flight attendants would remember them from the flight.

This was from a Marine named Jim (last name withheld):

"15 Feb 68
Dear Patti
Hi! You probably don't remember me, but that is a small problem because I'll never forget you. . . My name is Jim (last name withheld). I was on your flight from Norton to Alaska in January.
    You might remember this, four of us receive good luck kisses and helped you make coffee. Does that ring a bell? Hope so, because I was the only one that got your address. And a promise to go for a ride on your boat when I get out of the service in July.
16 Feb
Hi again, something came up so I couldn't finish this letter yesterday. Charly started playing games again.
I'm just about six foot, will be twenty-three in Oct. I love wild parties, but don't get me wrong I have nothing against a quiet evening with a beautiful young lady."
    Jim wrote that he planned on attending college and would make another try at professional racing. He said he tried once and ruined his car in his ninth race. The letter ended with, "So be good and write soon
                              Love
                              Luck
                              Laughter Jim."

*   *   *   *   *

On January 5, 1968, Samuel (last name withheld) an Army medic and staff sergeant wrote Patti. At the end of the letter one sees the "routine" of daily events in the combat zone.

"Patti, I think we have two things in common you were adopted by a family (Patti said she was "adopted" by neighbors in her home town wherever she went) and you are lonely or seem to be. I am in the same boat. I would like to know you better and possibly make a life partnership out of it. By the way, I am the sergeant that was supposed to give you one of my unit crests to remember me by. I will send you one in the near future. Must go to work and patch the wounded men.
A friend
Sammy J"

*   *   *   *   *

Sometimes letters from young soldiers or Marines revealed such honesty and need that flight attendants felt compelled to continue the correspondence. This was the case for Judy Vaughn, a 26-year-old angel in the air who was disguised as a Flying Tiger flight attendant.

Judy Vaughn 1968

On February 10, 1998, Vietnam veteran David Schumacher E-mailed the Flying Tiger Pilots' Association telling them about a flight he was on two days before Christmas in 1968. The trip was from McChord AFB in Washington to Vietnam.

Schumacher, who went to Vietnam as an Army Private First Class wrote, "My name is David Schumacher. Flying Tigers Airlines flew me to Vietnam in 1968 and back to the states in 1969. On the flight over, a flight attendant named Judy Vaughn befriended me and made me feel like what we were doing was something worthwhile. Judy and I wrote the whole year I was over there. She is a very special person to me and always will be for making me feel more comfortable in that environment. She was truly an angel and someone her employer should have been proud of. Now after 30 years I would like to thank her for what she did and just see how she is doing now.

I don't have much information, except her last letter, which was to me in Vietnam, October 1969. Would you please e-mail me back to let me know if there is any way I could get my address to her or anyone who knows her to communicate after all these years?

You guys did a wonderful job and my heartfelt thanks go to you all. God bless you all. David."

* * * * *

Former Flying Tiger Pilot George Gewehr contacted David immediately. Judy Vaughn was a favorite of his and the two are shown in the cockpit of a Tiger 747.

Captain George Gewehr and
Flight Attendant Judy Vaughn 1968

George Gewehr regretfully informed David Schumacher that Judy
Vaughn had passed away three years earlier at the age of 54.

On February 11, 1998, Gewehr's wife, Julie who was a flight attendant
for Flying Tiger Line after being with Pacific Southwest Airlines (PSA) sent
this message:

Julie Gewehr

"Hi David: I'm Julie Gewehr, longtime friend of Judy, 30 plus years.
Judy is responsible for me getting a job with Tigers, then meeting my
husband in Anchorage on my first trip with them and on to Nam. Judy is one
of those unforgettable people and she left many broken hearts when she

died. She shouldn't have died so young, nor in such an agonizing way. She was very brave and never gave up hope, though it didn't ever look very hopeful for her (breast cancer, or lung, not sure of the source).

"She fought for 2 1/2 years and died just before Thanksgiving at home in Alpine, CA. (Just east of San Diego.) Her husband, Larry and her mother were there. Her funeral was totally planned by Judy. She selected her gravesite here in San Diego at El Camino Memorial Park. The service was beautiful and the music, everything just lovely. We all left to walk up to the gravesite; lots of people, and just then the Navy jets from Miramar flew directly overhead, low, and in a tight formation. We all looked up and someone said, "Judy, you thought of everything." She was like that, as you know, and always thought of everyone else. She was incredibly loyal. Judy would want you to never forget her and hold your memory of her in your heart. She would like that. I know I always will. She touched literally hundreds of lives. Go ahead and send your tribute. Nice to hear from you and lovely to know that Judy is remembered so beautifully. Best wishes to you and your family, Julie Gewehr."

* * * * *

On February 13, 1998, David Schumacher's message about his flight to Vietnam and meeting Judy was sent to Flying Tigers.

"On this flight I met a most remarkable person. Her name was Judy Vaughn. I remember that Judy got on the flight in Japan. I had called home for the last time . . . and was feeling less than good about things. On the flight, Judy and I struck up a conversation. I remember after the flight attendants served us those wonderful hot dogs and Cokes, I went to the back galley and we just started talking. She was a most interesting person, very calm, very sure of herself listening to me, yet every now and then questioning me about things. But the most important thing I remember about Judy was her total calming effect on me. She impressed me as someone who cared about some stranger going to a land full of grief, danger and unrest. We talked for hours it seemed unless she had to go do her job.

"One thing I remember so vividly . . . she told me that Christmas could be worshipped anywhere, any place, even in Vietnam with all the turmoil, death and destruction going on. The calming effect still literally came out of her every word. She was my angel, someone sent to me in such a time of need. I will never forget that and never want to. I didn't want to get off that airplane; I was so nervous, scared and unsure of things. Then Judy came up to me shortly before it was my turn to get in line to get off and slipped a piece of paper in my shirt pocket. She only said, 'Here, I want you to have this.' I knew what I hoped it was, but didn't look; I only looked at her, smiled and then walked off that airplane to a war.

"Because of that one piece of paper, with her address on it, I am a much better person. I got to communicate with a wonderful person, one who showed human compassion, caring, and so many other beautiful attributes. We wrote back and forth the whole year and I got to know many of her feelings about the war and those who were fighting in it.

"During that year, in her letters, I detected a change. The trips back and forth to that dismal place were wearing her down. A very gentle sadness was creeping in. She tried hard to keep it out, but it was there. But Judy kept writing, so faithfully, so regularly, and I so looked forward to seeing her letters.

"She and I had planned on a short meeting after my return but it never happened. We wrote some after I got back to the states and then, over the years, our communication dwindled.

"Now to the present. In the process of moving this week, I found a box in my attic, full of Vietnam letters and other items from the war. Still bundled together, was a stack of letters from Judy.

I thought I need to try and find her now, even after all these years, to thank her for making my year in Vietnam more bearable, more sensible, more livable.

I was stunned when George Gewehr answered my e-mail inquiry about Judy. After emotions subsided I decided to do what Judy would have done, to help keep something alive, which was so beautiful and so wonderful."

* * * * *

David then attached a tribute to Judy written by his mother, Liz Schumacher on August 24, 1969, shortly after David returned from Vietnam and 26 years before Judy Vaughn Curtis died.

Mrs. Schumacher's words included these thoughts:

"Wherever a band of angels is gathered doing what their God has designated, there will be a Judy in their midst . . . Who but Judy could assure him (the lonely soldier) that Christmas could be worshipped wherever in the far world one happens to me and who but Judy could have reached out to him in his fear and anxiety, and handed him the God he so loved and needed and Who might also seem so far away?"

"Who but Judy should think of him in her busy hours and take time to send him reassurance in a tiny envelope, large with all the things he needed to know . . . remembrance, sincerity, friendship, beauty.
Who but Judy could encourage him to do his job well. . . God has need of such as these and may His brightest smile and His richest blessing go ahead of Judy, to light her way because. . .Judy fills her requirements with all the Christian, lady-like love that goes to make up what she is and what she does. . . 'Inasmuch as ye have done it until the least of these, ye have done it unto Me.'"

* * * * *

Not all letters during that time were from military men stationed in Vietnam. In late 1965, Patti Medaris received a Christmas card from Pensacola, Florida with a letter enclosed from Navy Lieutenant Frank Gallagher. She had met him at Luke Air Force outside of Phoenix, Arizona in 1965 where he was stationed. His letter was written December 13, 1966 telling her that six weeks earlier he had been selected to be part of the Navy's elite Blue Angels precision flying team.

He wrote, "Needless to say I was overjoyed. I have been flying for about one week now. We will practice here in Pensacola during December and then will leave on 10 January for winter training in El Centro, California of all places. El Centro is really in the boondocks.

Got to go now.

Thanks for the letters.

Write soon.

Frank"

F-11A Tiger

Two months later on February 1, 1967, after just six weeks with the Blue Angels, Frank Gallagher was killed when his Grumman F-11A Tiger jet crashed in the desert 16 miles northwest of the Naval Air Facility. He was flying solo in a four-man formation and the No. 6 spot in the full team formation when his plane spun into the ground.

Chapter 6
Stars and Stripes, ROK Marines and a Scary General

Flight attendants remembered "*Stars and Stripes* runs. These were flights in Southeast Asia that brought the military newspaper to troops in Vietnam, the Philippines, Japan and South Korea.

Created during the Civil War, the daily newspaper distributed around the world, reports on general news but with an emphasis on the military. It is funded by the Department of Defense, advertising and subscriptions and while it has First Amendment protection, it has had to deal with critics who believed coverage sometimes was slanted in favor of military brass.

Pacific *Stars and Stripes* December 14, 1968

World Airways flight attendant Janet Bancroft (Burttram) remembers, "World carried soldiers all over Southeast Asia during the war. Mostly to/from Vietnam but we also did the *Stars and Stripes* run which carried soldiers within Korea, many stops later ending in Bangkok, Thailand. In Korea we went to Pusan, Osan, Taegu, Kimpo, etc. The plane was a 727 with cargo (including bound stacks of *Stars and Stripes* newspapers) in the front half and 48 passengers in the aft. We had to carry coffee to the cockpit through the cargo in a darkened plane. Some gals didn't like it, but it was actually fun and those were the trips where every once in a while, even though it was technically against regulations, we could take off or land in the cockpit."

An alternative to *Stars and Stripes* was *Overseas Weekly*, a newspaper that began publishing in 1950 in Frankfurt, Germany. There were frequent conflicts with the military establishment over the paper's coverage of courts martial or editorial content that was deemed too racy for the *Stars and Stripes*. Some called the paper Oversexed Weekl*y*. During the height of the Vietnam War, space for the publication was refused at military newsstands in South Vietnam. In 1966 *Overseas Weekly* was printed in Hong Kong and flown to Saigon each week. The publication ceased operations in 1975.

* * * * *

For Patti Medaris (Culea), while with Airlift International she remembers the *Stars and Stripes* runs but also has vivid and eye-watering memories flying into Kimpo Air Base near Soul, South Korea to pick up Republic of Korea (ROK) Marines and take them to South Vietnam.

"We picked up the ROK Marines in Kimpo," she says. "Every one of them carried a jar of kimchi (salted and fermented cabbage, radishes, scallions, garlic, ginger, and jeotgal). They smelled garlicky but that's when I learned to eat kimchi."

Although she knew the ROK Marines had a reputation of being tough she said they were very polite.

"They were all in uniform and ready to go to 'work.' There was always an interpreter on board but many of the ROK Marines spoke English. Unlike American soldiers and Marines, the ROK Marines never asked us for kisses and if we were near and they used strong language they would say, 'Excuse me ma'am.' On the trip they played a lot of cards."

* * * * *

The ROK Marines were legendary for their courage and ferocity in combat during the Vietnam War.

It was known that they would beat their own troops to an inch of their lives for the slightest infraction, so when it came time to engage the enemy their battlefield performance came with an overall kill ratio of 25-to-1. On the downside, the ROK Marines were known to commit atrocities, often on civilian villagers.

The Koreans arrived in South Vietnam shortly after the U.S. Marines landed in 1965 and stayed and fought until the end in 1973. At their peak, they had close to 50,000 boots on the ground. More than 300,000 served and about 5,000 died.

* * * * *

Patti Medaris (Culea) also remembers military brass that flew on Airlift International and one four-star officer in particular.

"General Creighton Abrams was one we had often. He flew from Yokota to Da Nang and Saigon," she said.

(Army General Creighton Abrams commanded military operations in the Vietnam War from 1968 to 1972)

General Creighton Abrams

"The first time I had General Abrams on a flight he didn't like the way we were serving him his meal. He scared us, as he was really gruff. But that changed when he found out my name and asked me if I were related to General Medaris."

Major General John B. Medaris
U.S. Army photo

(John Bruce Medaris was Patti's great uncle. He was a highly decorated retired Army Major General from World War II who served in every campaign from North Africa to Sicily, Normandy, the Battle of the Bulge, and the invasion of Germany. He later played a key role in America's early space program and after retirement became an ordained Episcopal priest.)

"When he learned I was related to General Medaris," Patti said, "He then softened. The other girls thanked me because he had all of us uptight."

* * * * *

Part of the flight attendants' duties during the Vietnam War was to work on trips that carried civilians. They ranged from South Vietnamese locals to dependents of military personnel.

World Airways flight attendant Janet Bancroft (Burttram) recalls many trying moments with the locals.
"We flew Vietnamese civilians, every other day from Saigon to Da Nang, off-loaded them and then returned to Saigon with local civilian passengers picked up in Da Nang, off-load them, then take more passengers from Saigon to Hue, then Hue back to Saigon, then one more round-trip at the end

of the day to Da Nang. So, it was Saigon, Da Nang, Saigon, Hue, Saigon, Da Nang and Saigon. We had two South Vietnamese flight attendants on board and they handled the communications and made the announcements etc."

"The passengers were peasants. Most had never been on a plane. They didn't know what a lavatory was. We had to block off one of the two front lavs for the crew. The other three were for the passengers. They peed in the sink, didn't lock the doors, squatted over the john, etc. Some just peed on the walls. They came onboard with their goats and chickens. The babies didn't have diapers. There were families of five and six all crowded together in a row for three. (We were supposed to apply FAA rules...forget it).
After the first day we had to cover the carpet down the aisle of the plane and used yellow tarps. That was a big mistake because yellow was a sacred color for Buddhists and caused some aggravation. But we needed to do it because of the urine and liquids etc. getting ground into the carpet.
We served them a meal. It was a piece of chicken, a hard-boiled egg and a small Dixie cup of room temperature tea. I remember two ladies with black teeth (we think from chewing beetle nuts) who we took to Da Nang in the morning and returned with them on board in the afternoon run. They would go up with full bags and come back empty. They were dealing on the black market. They showed us their wares and it was all G.I. items: batteries, toothpaste and magazines, Kleenex etc. You could find all of this stuff for sale from street vendors in Saigon."

Chapter 7
Rest & Recuperation

Part of the Military Airlift Command (MAC) contract was flying troops to ten locations for Rest and Recuperation (R and R). In order to qualify for those trips, soldiers, sailors, Marines and airmen had minimum time limits for being in the combat zone (in-country requirements) that ranged from three to ten months.

Three months in country earned a visit to Bangkok, Thailand, Hong Kong, Manila, Singapore and Taipei. If a serviceman were in country for six months, they could take a break in Tokyo, Hawaii, Penang and Kuala Lumpur. A trip to Sydney, Australia was given to those who were in the combat zone for ten month.

For a brief time the troops could wear civilian clothes, something Patti Medaris (Culea) remembers.
"The R & R flights were notable because the guys wore civvies (civilian clothes). I don't know where they bought them but they all dressed similarly in plaid or checked shirts and kakis. And of course they had short military haircuts. Back in the 'real world' the trend was long hair so they didn't exactly blend in while on leave."

Flight attendants working those trips were able to give the troops a taste of home. Janet Bancroft (Burttram) knew the smiles she would see.
"When I flew with World we had just taken over the R & R flights to Sydney from Vietnam. On those trips the guys got steak, salad, apple pie and ice cream."
But she also saw the effects of the war on soldiers, sailors, airmen and Marines.
"It was nighttime. We told them if they were going to sleep but wanted to be awakened to eat, to leave their tray tables down. Which, they did. I approached one guy whose table was down, and I tapped him lightly on the shoulder to waken him. He jumped up so fast and briefly had his hands around my neck. Luckily he woke up and I realized this was just a natural reaction to what they have been through."

* * * * *

Patti Medaris (Culea) remembers warnings that were given to troops on R& R flights. "I learned a lot about sexually transmitted diseases on our R&R flights. When we'd arrive in Bangkok a sergeant would come on board, get on the PA and give the 'talk' about what to look out for, how to avoid contracting a Sexually Transmitted Disease (STD) and what clubs to stay away from (that was really stupid as you know those were the ones they went to), and how to represent America. Good advice, but I'm not sure if it sunk in much."

* * * * *

Flight attendant Jeannie Wagers (Wiseman) was on R & R trips from Vietnam to Sydney, Australia only she said the destination was not referred to as Rest and Relaxation.

"The men called it I & I," she said. (Intoxication and Intercourse)

Photos Courtesy: BJ Elliott
Behind My Wings

* * * * *

Nancy (Wood) Shamel, a flight attendant for World Airways on the World Airways Alumni website remembers flying a lot with fellow flight attendant Carol Papetti on R & R trips.

Nancy (Wood) Shamel
Courtesy World Airways

"We had a little game we played. We would go through the plane and check out which handsome guy we wanted to visit with. We usually ended up picking the same guy.

"So, competition began, who was going to be the one to get his attention and keep it? I can still remember the guy. Carol was working the front of the plane and I was in the back, but the nicest looking Green Beret was sitting in the very front seat across from the jump seat. Carol had a head start on me but in the end I won. In fact, when we picked up the plane the next morning in Darwin from Sydney, the crew that had relieved us the day before asked, 'which of you gals is Nancy, that handsome Green Beret fell in love with you.'"

Nancy recalled another memory with Carol Papetti September 7,1968 on a flight from Bien Hoa, Vietnam.

"When I walked from the cockpit to the back galley," she said, "all 168 soldiers on board looked at me as I passed them and smiled or chuckled. When I got to the galley I asked my dear friend Carol 'do I have a button on my blouse undone or is something else wrong with my uniform or me?' With a very straight face she said 'no.' I made another trip to the front and back again and got the same chuckles and smiles. I decided to check the back of my uniform myself this time. Stuck to my rear was a piece of paper, on this piece of paper was written - WATCH ME WIGGLE - the navigator (Ray Vandeven) had written this and put it on my rear when I was in the cockpit. The plane was full of laughter when I finally discovered this, so I said, 'Ok guys you want to watch me wiggle?' I went up the aisle swinging my hips from one side of the seats to the other. The soldiers loved it."

* * * * *

There were pleasant surprises awaiting flight attendants when they flew into Bangkok. Patti Medaris (Culea) remembers them well. "On our deadhead flights from Clark Air Force Base in the Philippines to Bangkok to pick up R & R guys to take them back to Vietnam, as soon as we landed a van would pull up next to the plane and open its side doors. Inside the van were all kinds of alcohol, Scotch, Drambuie, rum, vodka, etc. selling for $2 a quart.

"There was a lot of drinking during this time. It was stress relief. Having had alcohol poisoning in 1966, I couldn't drink that much. Thank goodness! So, I was always the designated leader to make sure we got to our hotel when we'd arrive in Bangkok. On deadheading without passengers, the pilots didn't drink, but the crew in the back had more than their fill."

An R & R trip for the troops also meant a break for flight attendants and for Patti Medaris (Culea) her favorite layover was Bangkok, Thailand.

Patti Medaris (Culea)
Wearing clothing made in Bangkok

"We were able to have clothes tailor made for us," she remembers wistfully. "All you needed was to bring in a photo of what you wanted. They would measure you and two days later we could go pick it up. They were beautifully made for practically nothing."

Some of those clothes were carried in a special garment bag that Patti had custom made in Okinawa that she still uses today.

* * * * *

World Airways flight attendant Lorna McLearie and two of her colleagues also bought garment bags in Okinawa.

"I was a little bit of a rebel," she admits, "and had peace signs placed under our names for the three of us. No one said anything and as time wore on everyone was more relaxed and allowed our personalities to show."

* * * * *

World Airways flight attendant Jeannie Wagers (Wiseman) had her favorite shopping destinations.

"We got our shoes made in Korea. Bangkok was good for jewelry and Thai silk and the Philippines had lots of wood," she said.

* * * * *

JoAnn Wright (Wintenburg) also looks back with fondness on her Asian shopping experiences.

"Hawaii, Guam, the Philippines and Okinawa had an economic boost with the crews laying over in those places. We came home with so many fun things. I still have my monogramed garment bags, monkey pod plates and salad bowls that we bought over there. We would sightsee, get our hair done, get massages on our layovers and then all meet for happy hour and dinner at the end of the day.

"I met the Blue Angles on a Mobile, Alabama MAC layover thanks to our First Officer Dave Hicks who was friends with them. We also got to meet the SR-71 pilots on their stays in Okinawa. They loved the crews and we loved them but I specifically remember my first hangover with those guys having taken us to one of the O Clubs. The staffs at the hotels were so nice and tolerated the partying crews with much patience. Many relationships began with our girls and the military and some with the pilots. War was Hell but we crews managed to make good times out of it."

* * * * *

"Fussa was a mini shopping mecca for us," says Janet Bancroft (Burttram). "They had Papasan chairs and electronics including stereos, speakers, radios, cameras, etc. You name it, they had it and we bought it! The crews lugged back all sorts of goodies. And Saigon was great, too."

Janet Bancroft (Burttram) shopping in Saigon

* * * * *

The emotional drain on flight attendants of taking troops to war and bringing them back home was balanced somewhat by adventures few people could imagine. Layovers for the crews in the Philippine Islands included a boat trip down a river.

JoAnn Wright (Wintenburg) with her Continental colleagues 1971

JoAnn riding a bicycle at the Okinawa Officer's Rest Center
Note: The photo caption in the *Stars and Stripes* newspaper today would be politically incorrect. It read:
"BICYCLING AND GIRL WATCHING ARE POPULAR AT THE

OKUMA REST CENTER"

* * * * *

Flying Tiger Line flight attendant Lydia Cowgill (Rossi) had clothes made in Japan and shopped in Saigon and the Philippines. She still has one of her treasured silk dresses.

Lydia Cowgill (Rossi) 1965   2019
Wearing a silk dress bought in Saigon

* * * * *

In December 1970, while with Airlift International, Patti Medaris (Culea) had a layover in Bangkok and went with her flight attendant friends to a performance of the Ink Spots at the Dusit Thani Hotel. Little did she know that she would soon meet actress Raquel Welch who was traveling with Bob Hope's USO tour.

The Ink Spots   Bob Hope and Raquel Welch

"I had watched the first show with my friends and since I loved the Ink Spots, I decided to see the second show. My friends took off and I was alone when I looked up and there was Raquel Welch standing by my table. She said, 'I see your friends have left. Would you mind if I joined you?' I recognized her immediately and after getting over the initial shock I said, of course.

"She told me the Ink Spots were her favorite group and just like that we began talking as if we were long friends. She was a very real person and we found we had one thing in common and that was Mr. Hope. When I worked for Bonanza Airlines, he was often on our flights into Palm Springs."

And what did her friends say after she told them whom she had met? "They didn't believe me," she said, "and I didn't get her autograph."

Later that month, Patti and her crewmates saw the Bob Hope Christmas show at Da Nang. Did she try to meet again with Raquel Welch?

"No," she says with a laugh. "We were hundreds of yards from the stage, which is just as well. The show was for the boys, not us."

* * * * *

A year earlier, Flying Tiger flight attendant Marsha Hay (Merz) was in Da Nang on Christmas Day when the Bob Hope show was performing.

" I've only ever missed one Christmas with my family," Marsha said. "I flew a Flying Tiger troop flight in and out of Da Nang on Christmas Day 1969. The Bob Hope show was performing in Da Nang on that day. The troops that boarded our flight told us that they would rather see us than the Bob Hope show. They were happy and excited to be going home."

* * * * *

Note: From May 1965-June 1972 there were 569 USO shows with 5,600 performances in Vietnam.

* * * * *

While Bob Hope was the person most associated with the USO shows during the Vietnam War, there were other entertainers who gave their time and talent to support the troops. One of them was the late Don Ho. He was an Air Force veteran and performed with Bob Hope but also honored military personnel in his own shows.

World Airways flight attendant Jeannie Wagers (Wiseman) recalls the time when Don Ho coaxed her and the flight attendants she was with to come up on stage to sing their parody of Roger Miller's hit song "Oh, Lonesome Me."

It seems that Roger Miller was flying Continental and got so angry with them he walked off their plane in Okinawa and Jeannie and her flight attendant friends met him at the hotel. Later they took his music and adapted it to "Oh, horny me."

Jeannie continues the story. "Some fool told Don Ho that we knew this song and we started to leave his show and he had us carried on stage to sing it. I said, 'no way.' But Ho looked at the audience and said, 'Come on folks, give these Pan Am stews a big hand and we'll have them sing.'"

(He knew Jeannie and her friends were with World but said Pan Am to protect them.)

So, Jeannie and her fellow flight attendants got up and sang the following:
  "Everybody's going out and gettin' some,
    and I'm sittin' home getting' none.
    Somebody put the make on me,
    Oh, horny me."

Jeannie Wagers (Wiseman) and Don Ho

A final chapter to the story was still to come.

"Next day on the flight," Jeannie said, "there was a chaplain looking at me and really staring at me. Finally he said, 'you look familiar. I think I've seen you before.'

Jeannie quickly replied, "Well, it certainly was not me at the Don Ho show," and walked off."

* * * * *

While rules and regulations were usually followed to the letter, there were times when looking the other way fit the occasion, especially on R & R runs.

Janet Bancroft (Burttram) of World Airways recalled one of them.

"We picked up a planeload of GI's from Vietnam on their way to Sydney for R & R. They were a fun group. We left them at the airport in Darwin and went to our hotel but were called back to serve them lunch on the aircraft because of a mechanical problem. We were already out of uniform and tired. Our senior flight attendant said no problem, don't put the uniform back on so we served them while wearing our shorts and tops. They had been drinking beer at the terminal and were in a good mood. Let's face it; they were about to have a week away from Vietnam! So they helped us run the trays and serve coffee etc. Everyone had fun. We were the same crew who took them back to Vietnam when they returned from Sydney. That didn't happen very often."

Chapter 8
The December Curse

The numbers support that it is far safer to be in a commercial airplane than an automobile. According to the National Safety Council, Americans have a 1 in 114 chance of dying in a car crash compared to a 1 in 9,821 while in an airplane, which includes private flights and air taxis. Even though some airline meals make you gag, those chances are almost three times better than meeting your fate by choking on food.

With that said, Flying Tiger Line went through a horrible time from 1962 to 1966 when four of its planes went down in the month of December. Another plane crashed in March of 1966. Understandably, with that history in mind, there was apprehension for pilots and flight attendants when December rolled around.

The first accident happened on December 14, 1962 when Flying Tiger Line Flight 183, an L-1049H Super Constellation crashed on approach to Lockheed Air Terminal in Burbank, California. The pilot suffered a suspected heart attack and all five on board and three on the ground were killed.

A second fatal crash on Christmas Eve 1964 happened when Flying Tiger Line Flight 282, a Lockheed Super Constellation crashed in heavy fog and rain shortly after take-off from San Francisco International Airport. It was bound for JFK International Airport in New York carrying cargo of electronic equipment, bolts of fabric, women's scarves, bandannas, purses and costume jewelry for the Christmas holiday.
    The pilot asked the tower for permission to change his radio setting from take-off to departure frequency and shortly after that, the plane crashed near the top of a ridge in San Bruno, killing all three crew members.

A third December crash happened on the 15th of that month in 1965 when Flying Tiger Line Flight 914, an L-1049H Super Constellation out of Los Angeles bound for Chicago struck California Peak near Alamosa, Colorado after the pilot did not make a Southeast turn in IFR conditions, killing the three crew members.

The worst crash for Flying Tiger Line happened December 24, 1966 when a four-engine Canadair CL-44 cargo plane with military clothing from Japan encountered a down burst and wind shear and went below the glide slope while attempting a radar-controlled night approach landing in heavy rain at the Da Nang air base. Four crew members and 125 Vietnamese villagers of a tiny hamlet were killed. American Marines nearby were called to recover bodies.

* * * * *

The most mysterious crash happened March 16, 1962. This was three years before American boots were on the ground in South Vietnam, but our involvement in the region had been secretly building. On that day, Flying Tiger Line Flight 739, a Lockheed L-1049 Super Constellation from Travis Air Force Base in California was on its final leg to Saigon with 93 U.S. soldiers and three South Vietnamese when it disappeared over the Western Pacific Ocean.

A Lockheed Constellation L-1049 similar to the Flying Tiger aircraft lost.

The 93 American troops were jungle-trained Army Rangers, primarily highly trained electronics and communications specialists. The other three were members of the armed forces of Vietnam. There was a multi-member flight crew on board, used by the company when it wanted the trip to keep moving. It consisted of three pilots, two flight engineers, two navigators and four flight attendants, Senior Flight Attendant Barbara Jean Walmsley from Santa Barbara, California; Hildegard Muller; Christel Diana Reiter of San Mateo; and Patricia Wassum.

Author Sylvia Wrigley, who has written extensively about why planes crash offers insight on Flight 739 in a September 30, 2016 column.

She notes that Flight 739 had stopped in Honolulu, Wake Island and Guam. The last transmission from the aircraft was about 90 minutes out of Guam. It was then that a Liberian tanker reported seeing a bright light in the sky near the aircraft's expected position after the last radio contact.

The ship's crew said they noticed something similar to a vapor trail slightly north of the tanker moving in an east-to-west direction. The vapor trail passed behind a cloud and then there was an intense explosion of two pulses, lasting two to three seconds. The crew believed they saw two flaming objects of equal brightness and size plummet at two different speeds, into the sea. As they fell, a crewmember noticed a small bright target on the ship's radar, bearing 270 degrees at a range of 17 miles.

The captain of the tanker said he saw the fall of the slower object before it disappeared into the sea. He ordered the ship's course reversed and for five and a half hours searched the area but found no trace of wreckage or debris. Unable to contact the U.S. Navy radio stations at Manila and Guam, the captain thought the explosion was a military exercise and resumed his ship's course.

When Flight 739 failed to arrive in Saigon, a massive search by aircraft and surface ships from four branches of the U.S. military was launched. It covered more than 200,000 square miles but after eight days when no trace of the aircraft was found, the search was called off and to this day, nothing from Flight 739 has ever turned up.

The investigation, not universally supported, supposedly revealed that the flight line and ramp areas at Honolulu, Wake Island and Guam were not secure and anyone could have entered and had access to non-military aircraft parked at the airfields. Specifically at Guam, the last stop, the aircraft was left unattended in a dimly lit area for some time.

Adding to the intrigue and bolstering those who believe the real story was covered up was that an identical Lockheed Super Constellation departed Travis Air Force Base on the same day for Kadena Air Force Base, Okinawa, Japan. Flight 7816 was carrying a heavy load; possibly a ship's drive shaft and unknown to the crew there were corrosives, paint and batteries on board. Several hours later when the aircraft approached Adak, Alaska in the Aleutian Islands, it encountered difficulties. The pilot appeared to have issues on the instrument approach and crashed short of the runway.

The investigation revealed the airliner was below the glide path and despite seven separate warnings from the ground controller, the airplane's landing gear struck rocks 328 feet short of the runway threshold and slid for 2,000 feet along the runway coming to rest just off its edge. The main landing gear was torn off. Seven crewmembers survived with minor injuries but flight engineer James Johnstone was trapped in the cockpit. The fuselage sat there for some time but then a fire started in the tail section but Johnstone, unable to free himself, died in the fire.

One of the reasons for not accepting the conclusions of government investigators in the disappearance of Flight 739 is the political climate at the time. George Gewehr, a former Flying Tiger Line pilot and current historian for the Flying Tiger Line Pilots' Association opines that President John F. Kennedy wanted the public to believe he was decreasing American involvement in Vietnam whereas he was sending in more troops.

"After our Tiger people returned from talking to the tanker's crew," Gewehr says, "they felt the airplane was shot down."

Gewehr and others suspect a Sidewinder Missile, known to go off on their own, did just that from a Navy jet fighter and sent the Flying Tiger airliner to its doom.

Adding to that theory, says Gewehr, are words from President Kennedy's press secretary Pierre Salinger.

Salinger, who passed away in 2004, went public in 1996 saying he believed a Navy missile went awry and brought down TWA Flight 800 off Long Island on July 17, 1996, killing 230 persons on board. Investigators concluded a spark inside the plane ignited a fuel tank in the 747 but eight years later Salinger publicly disagreed.

Gewehr says, " I think Salinger said that about the TWA disaster because he knew a Navy missile brought down the Tiger Flight 739 plane. He repeated something that no one else wanted known."

There is also the issue of the fuel tank on the TWA 747.

"I flew the 747 for 15 years," says Gewehr, "and never once was there any feeling of a fuel tank might explode. Tigers had some very old 100-model 747's and you could smell the fuel fumes when they put fuel in the center tank but never once did we ever have a problem with it. I flew copilot and captain on the Constellation (the same L-1049 Tiger aircraft that went down) and never did I feel or have any knowledge of one exploding in flight. The Super Connie was a proven airplane and reliable."

Gewehr and relatives of those killed on Tiger Air Line Flight 739 believe some sort of recognition for their sacrifice is due the men and women who lost their lives on that flight over the Pacific. Many believe the 93 Army Rangers killed on the flight should have their names engraved on the Vietnam Wall.

"No one in the government wants to address the problem," Gewehr says. "This has been going on now for a very long time and the relatives are dying off."

Looking back on what happened in 1962, Gewehr recalls the words of Robert Prescott, founder of the Flying Tiger Line.

"He said the 1962 year was the 'Year of the Tiger' on the Chinese calendar and we were going to have a great year. Needless to say, it was just the opposite."

Chapter 9
Souvenirs

Letters from soldiers and Marines were not the only memories flight attendants had of the troops who they had flown to war. There were times when the young men wanted to leave part of themselves with the friendly faces who had been their last connection with home. Some of them gave their uniform, insignia ranks and company patches.

Today, Patti Medaris (Culea) can slip on the Army uniform shirt given to her by a soldier on his way to Vietnam. She also has several shoulder patch insignias and PFC chevrons and two captain's bars.

The uniform shirt was a size Small and belonged to a Private First Class soldier whose last name was Fleischmann. On the left shoulder was a blue, red and white patch for what then was the United States Fifth Army. In 2004 the Fifth Army became the Army Service Component Command of the U.S.

Northern Command.

Another soldier in Vietnam gave Patti an ammunition belt used to feed cartridges into a firearm. While this book was being written, two friends told us that several of the cartridges had live ammo.

You might think that the soldiers and Marines would have given parts of their uniform going home but the opposite happened.

"The boys on the flight home were entirely different than they were on the trip to Vietnam," she said. "Going to war they were loud and boisterous with a sense of bravado and gave away their rank insignias and other parts of their uniform. But coming home, the plane was usually quiet. Buddies had been killed and lives were changed forever and there was a sense of uncertainty about what they would face at home and how they would cope."

Flight attendant Leslie Laird (Pfeifer) in a 2014 newspaper story remembered being given something more personal than rank insignia or unit patches.

"The majority of them were drafted, enlisted 18-year-old GIs," she said. "You could tell they didn't want to be there. They were afraid. After I talked to one of them for a while he said, 'Here, I want you to have this.' "He gave me his rosary beads.

"I wasn't a Catholic, and I told him I couldn't accept them. He said, 'No, I want you to have them. I want to leave something.' He was going to the front lines, and he just knew he wasn't coming back."

* * * * *

Dick Scharff, a Navy supply lieutenant in 1966 saw first-hand and understood why Marines looked the way they did when it came time to go home.

Lt. Dick Scharff

"These kids, their uniforms were a mess, they didn't dress up for that hop out of Da Nang," he said. "They cleaned up pretty good when they sent them from Okinawa back to the states, but Da Nang to Okinawa, they didn't worry about an inspection."

What he remembers most though was the expression on the faces he saw when he was sent from Da Nang to Okinawa to find out why supplies such as barbed wire were being delayed in getting to the front lines.

"We took a plane load of Marines to Okinawa and the kids had a 'thousand-yard stare,'" he says.

The term comes from a painting by Tom Lea that first appeared in a 1945 *Life* magazine depicting a soldier with a blank, unfocused gaze who has become emotionally detached from the horrors around him.

Scharff could read the words on the Marines' faces and the "thousand-yard stare" needed no translation. To him the expressions silently asked, "'What have I done? Where have I been?' Trying to get over it."

* * * * *

Joan Policastro remembers notes from the troops that were left behind for her. On one flight, a young solider handed her a note that said not to read it until he left. When she opened it there were words of thanks and at the end of the letter he wrote, "I know I'm not coming home alive."

Another note that she has kept is folded in thirds and written on Pan Am stationery. Signed only "Rick," it offers his apologies for staring at her, wishes her well and offers hopes their paths might cross again. "I must say you look better than anything I've seen in 15 months in the Nam," he wrote.

Joan said these notes and seeing young draftees who wrote them "scared to death," led her to change her initial belief about Vietnam. She was totally against the war when it began but then had the belief that, "Well, if the government is in this war, it must be OK."

* * * * *

There were occasions when flight attendants were asked to give something to the troops besides their name and mailing address. Patti Medaris (Culea) and other flight attendants were asked to surrender their clothes, including intimate apparel. Patti recalls what happened on an especially long trip.

"We left Travis on January 30 for Anchorage and then Kadena. We then went back to LAX on February 2nd immediately flew from LAX to Travis, then Anchorage, Kadena and finally Da Nang.

Da Nang Air Base
Late 1960's

We had to wait there quite a while because the base was under attack. After things settled down, we visited a hospital and then met the Air Force guys at the base Flight Operations. It was quite a place with women's clothing hanging all over the walls.

"If you left everything, including underwear, you got a Tiger rug or a blanket."

Patti kept her panties but left an old Flying Tiger uniform.

"We were getting new uniforms, so I gave them the old one."

* * * * *

Jeannie Wagers (Wiseman) wanted to leave something that would not be forgotten but never was able to pull it off. "I was going to go to a store and get two bras and make a three-holder," she says with a laugh.

* * * * *

It wasn't until after the late 1960's that airlines began using portable food carts (trolleys) to bring drinks and meals to passengers. Vietnam-era flight attendants had to carry trays by hand.

Courtesy: *Behind My Wings*
BJ Elliott

"We could only carry two at a time," said Patti Medaris (Culea) because we were not allowed to stack them. As for drinks, I can only remember coffee, tea or milk—no soda pop."

Former flight attendant
Joan Policastro on board an R & R flight
Photo courtesy: *Reporter Newspapers*, John Ruch

Janet Bancroft (Burttram) recalls many trips up and down the aisles. "We 'ran' meals two at a time from the galley. Each soldier received a tray with an entree, beverage cup, plastic ware and napkin and probably a cookie or some kind for dessert. It was back and forth until all were fed. It was tiring especially on the longer flights because we might have two services. Once the meals were served we started with the coffee. We carried a pot until it emptied, then back for more. No decaf. No cocktails, soda, beer, etc. No water bottles back then.

"On the breakfast trays I remembered French toast with two little sausages and we included a carton of milk. Lunches were cellophane-wrapped ham and American cheese sandwiches. Ice cream came in a paper cup with a wooden spoon underneath. Strangely enough, we rarely had food left on anyone's plate as bad as it was. I'm pretty sure the military dictated the menus. Picking up the trays was much easier and didn't require as many trips. We could stack 3 or 4 trays (they were now lighter and flatter) and run them back to the galley. Sometimes it was overwhelming for the galley girl because she had to keep up with the mounds of trash and trays returning from the cabin. Nothing was reused except the trays. Recycling wasn't invented yet. If we had enough garbage bags we would put one in an empty bin and just dump everything but the main tray into the bin. It went much faster than having to slide each tray neatly back into a bin."

Patti Medaris (Culea) remembers food served on her flights. "Beef Burgundy was the favorite and we also had chicken."

Joan Policastro said that Pan Am's offerings were made with one thing in mind, "For the troops on the flights, Pan Am tried to have meals with a taste of home: steak, potatoes, ice cream and milk."

Janet Bancroft (Burttram) remembers what followed. "After the meal service sometimes we would set up a card table for guys who didn't want to sleep. We would pull out a couple of empty food and tray bins to use as chairs and tables and put a blanket over the one bin for a smooth surface on the make-shift table. Some of these guys could pass the time yucking it up trying to forget what's coming or what they left behind in Nam. One can only guess. We were just happy to be able to distract them or get them talking."

Janet Bancroft (Burttram) left, with a sailor and an unidentified flight attendant

"At the end of the flight," Janet said, "we had to go around during the approach and refold each blanket and put them back into the overhead rack. (No closable bins back then.) There was a blanket for each soldier. This was another of those times when every pair of eyes was watching the process of folding then replacing the blankets in the overhead rack; a little bit more leg was displayed, it couldn't be helped."

* * * * *

For security reasons, at the end of a trip when in Vietnam and the Philippines, flight attendants had to remain inside the aircraft while locals cleaned the cabin..

* * * * *

It was in the Philippine's that Patti Medaris (Culea) was given a lethal souvenir.

"When I was with Airlift I got to know Filipino natives who trained our military in jungle survival. When our troops were isolated for a training exercise, the Filipino natives would be secretly nearby observing them. I was invited by an Air Force helicopter pilot to go on a flight to check one of the training missions. On board was a Filipino commando there to make sure all was in order on the ground. As was the case with most of the natives he was short. He probably was in his 20's and spoke perfect English. I remember he had a kind face and could tell he took a liking to me. After about 30 minutes out of Clark Air Force Base, we circled over the training site and I think dropped a few supplies. We didn't stay too long before heading back to Clark and after we arrived, the Filipino on board gave me his silver Negrito Bolo sword that I still have. They were wonderful people, small in stature, but tall in courage."

"The sword is 21 inches long with a 15 ½-inch blade and has a couple of notches, supposedly for his kills. Some people have a gun for intruders," Patti says with a laugh. "We have my sword in the bedroom book case."

Negrito Bolo with two notches on the handle

* * * * *

Probably the most unusual "souvenir" taken out of the combat zone was seen by Overseas National Airways flight attendant Elisabeth Gyllman.

Elisabeth Gyllman
Honolulu 1967 and Cam Ranh Bay 1967

In 1967 Elisabeth was in Honolulu at a Waikiki Beach bar with another flight attendant, Marianne Missner.

Elisabeth was just 20 years old and having the time of her young life since leaving a small town in Sweden.

"Beside me sat a nice looking guy and we started talking," she wrote in an Overseas National Airways crew website. "He said he was on short leave from Vietnam for a couple of days. I was thrilled to pieces and couldn't quite grasp that you were in a war one day and then you got to leave to have holidays. I don't remember where he said he had been to fight but after a while he hauled a jar with some liquid in it from his pocket and set it on the bar. As I recall, the jar still had a brand name on it--a label, like a jar of peanut butter.

"'Do you know what this is?' he asked.

I looked and since it was rather dark in the room I couldn't make out what was floating in the jar.

"'This here is a Viet Cong ear,'" he said.

"He explained he had been in combat and had killed a Viet Cong guerilla soldier and had taken one ear as a kind of souvenir. I don't recall the guy's name, but the story stuck forever in my mind and I thought a lot about how he actually got that ear and still think about it often. The fear of dying makes you go almost insane. I can imagine being in combat and waiting to get killed or kill someone. It really had an impact on me, this happening in sunny Honolulu, sunshine paradise with leis and mai-tai's, far away from the war scene."

Chapter 10
Romance in the Air and on the Ground

When you have young ego-filled men and pretty young women together in a confined air space for hours at a time, there are bound to be romantic interludes that sometimes develop on the ground or in a few cases at 30,000 feet.

Former U.S. Army Special Forces and Specialist Five Army Green Beret, John Stryker "Tilt" Meyer has written three books about his combat service in Vietnam. He later became an award-winning newspaper reporter in San Diego County and was associate director in the veterans department at Interfaith Community Services in Escondido, California.

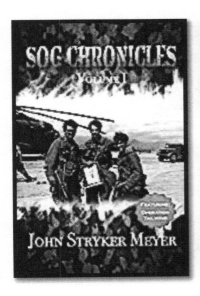 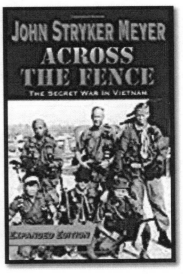

Lt.Gen. Richard Stillwell and "Tilt" 1969

John Stryker "Tilt" Meyer – 1968
(His nickname came as a boy playing pinball machines)

John remembers flying to Vietnam for his second tour of duty and while he can't recall the name of the airline, he has no problem bringing to mind two flight attendants who were on board.

"There were two stunning, bright flight attendants," Stryker Meyer said, " who, upon seeing our green berets treated us with extra kindness, drinks, food and sweet talk. My buddy ended up spending a few minutes in the rest room with one flight attendant for more intimate comfort and kindness."

John Stryker "Tilt" Meyer today

* * * * *

When asked about "The Mile High Club" a slang term for people who have had sex during a flight, Patti Medaris (Culea) says, "I never got talked into that, thankfully. In fact, I don't think I was ever asked. Just kisses."

* * * * *

A more traditional relationship happened between Flying Tiger Line pilot George Gewehr and his wife Julie Murtough (Gewehr) who was single and had just come over from Pacific Southwest Airways to work for Tigers.

"We met in Anchorage at the Captain Cook hotel. When we were on the airplane and taxiing out to take off, the senior flight attendant comes up to the cockpit and says one of the guys back there said there was a bomb on board. Guess what, it took three hours before we started for Tokyo and when we landed we were very late. The Captain said, 'George, I think it's time for a party, don't you' and I agreed. We had five extra stewardesses plus the regular amount so we went to the local bar and took them with us and one of them was Julie. When we left at 6 in the morning it had been snowing and Yokota air base was closed for three days. So we didn't go anywhere. I had separated from my then wife and living alone in Playa del Rey. We are coming up on our 50 years in knowing each other and 49 years of marriage. It has been some ride for sure."

George and Julie with son Jason, then a Navy Yeoman

Julie and George Gewehr

* * * * *

Jeannie Wagers (Wiseman) also married a pilot. John Wiseman, was a Marine Corps veteran who joined the Marines when he was 16 the day after Pearl Harbor was attacked. He flew as a private pilot before joining World Airways in 1960 and retired in 1994.

John Wiseman 1960's   2005

"John was first flying as co-pilot and then flight engineer," Jeannie remembers. "He and his pilot friends were chasing town girls and we got together after his third marriage."

John and Jeannie began seeing each other in 1976 and she remembers one night in particular.

"He came over to my house and we spent the next twelve hours talking," she said.

Jeannie says that her husband wasn't much of a talker, but not on this occasion.

"We drank a case of beer, one beer an hour."

They did not get married until 1978 but with it came a risk. At that time, flight attendants could not be married so Jeannie was fired from World Airways but not without a touch of irony from the airline owner Ed Daly.

"He gave us a wedding present," she says with a laugh.

Jeannie and John Wiseman
World Airways 1960's uniforms

* * * * *

Romance for Flying Tiger Line flight attendant Lydia Cowgill (Rossi) began in 1964.

Lydia Cowgill (Rossi)

It happened when one of the original American Volunteer Group (Flying Tigers) pilots walked into a bar in Palm Beach, Florida. He was 48-year-old John Richard Rossi, a Flying Tiger Line senior pilot who had downed six Japanese planes during World War II. In the room were fellow pilots and flight attendants on a layover.

John "Dick" Rossi 1940's   David Niven 1948   Dick Rossi 1966

"Dick came walking into the large room," Lydia remembers. "Somebody looked around and said, 'Oh, it's Dick Rossi.' He was in World War II and I heard of him. I looked at him and he came walking forward and I thought, 'He looks just like (actor) David Niven.' He saw me looking at him and he came right up to where I was standing and said hello to everybody and he said, 'Can I buy you all a drink?' I thought, 'how classy, I like that.' He kind of latched on to me."

Soon after, Dick and Lydia began dating. He had a home in Los Angeles and Lydia lived in San Francisco. The courtship continued and they planned to be married in April 1966. The only problem with that was that flight attendants could not be married.

Enter Flying Tiger Line founder and president Robert "Bob" Prescott who was Dick Rossi's longtime friend.

Bob Prescott, Greg Boyington and Dick Rossi, 1952
Photo: Flying Tigers Association

Dick Rossi and Lydia had asked to get three weeks off for their wedding and honeymoon.

"We were in his (Prescott's) office and Dick said, 'Lydia needs three weeks off and hasn't been approved."

Prescott then called the person in charge of scheduling and told him to come to his office.

Lydia remembers the man arriving soon. "It was a big office and I don't think the guy had ever been in the office before because he was very nervous. Bob looked at him and said, 'You were supposed to give Lydia a leave for her wedding.'"

Lydia says the man paused and then in a halting voice said, "Well, we have a rule that any stewardess who gets married has to quit."

Prescott quickly replied, "Well, I'm changing that."

In her interview with the author, Lydia's eyes sparkled and remembering the moment said, "Oh, that was great."

Robert Prescott, Dick and Lydia Rossi and Lydia's sister, Mary Lynn

Actually, Prescott was using a law passed two years earlier, the Civil Rights Act of 1964 that banned employment discrimination. Applying it to Lydia, she became the first flight attendant at Tigers (and possibly for any airline) who was able to work while married.

* * * * *

Continental flight attendant JoAnn Wright (Wintenburg) met her eventual husband Kenneth "Kip" Wintenburg when she was new on the job.

"He was a Second Officer when I met him working a MAC flight to Da Nang. I was 22 and he was 25."

After they began dating, although Wintenburg went by the nickname "Kip", flight attendant friend BJ Elliott (Prior) said the couple was referred to as "Ken" and "Barbie."

Kip Wintenburg   JoAnn Wright (Wintenburg)
      1968   1967

The relationship, shall we say, took off.

JoAnn (right) with the crew on a layover debriefing in Okinawa at the Kyoto Hotel - 1970

* * * * *

"We dated three years before we got married," she says, "and ended up being the longest pilot/flight attendant marriage before we retired."

JoAnn Wright (Wintenburg)
1972

Kip and JoAnn
1978

"He retired as a Boeing 777 Captain #1 on the seniority list in October 2004 with Continental," she says, "and I was #59 before Continental merged with United. We are going on 47 years married and 50 years together." And she adds for good measure, "We are still *in training*."

JoAnn and Kip   JoAnn and Kip today
1995

* * * * *

Sometimes marriages don't work. Such was the case for flight attendant Janet Bancroft and her first husband, an Air Force airmen she met in Seoul, Korea on a World Airways flight. In the photo below, Janet is shown on her wedding day with her good friend, Fredene Weaver (Maulhardt).

Janet Bancroft and Fredene Weaver (Maulhardt) at Janet's wedding in 1972.

While Janet's marriage ended after 14 years, her wedding dress (shown above) survived. She gave it to Fredene Weaver who used it to become Fredene Maulhardt in 1973.

Fredene Weaver (Maulhardt) and John Maulhardt

* * * * *

Janet Bancroft eventually found happiness and married George Burttram, a retired FBI Special Agent. Their travels over 23 years have taken them to Louisiana, Alaska, South Carolina, Virginia and now Florida.

Janet and George 1995 Janet Bancroft (Burttram) today

* * * * *

Patti Medaris (Culea) breathes a sign of relief when she remembers a close call on the romantic front.

"On one of my layovers in Bangkok," Patti says, "several of us went to a place called the Ahn Ahn Club. It was a huge hangout for military, but no 'bar' girls. It was a good place to meet other Americans and dance. That is where I met Air Force OV-10 Bronco pilot, John David Erickson."

John David "Eric" Erickson
Photo from: Friday Pilots

"Eric (that was his nickname and call sign) was there on R&R after being rescued by a Jolly Green Giant (the USAF HH-53 helicopter used in search and rescue operations). He showed me the boxer shorts the Jolly Green Giant crews give to those they rescue.

"He did a lot of secret stuff, which he couldn't talk about. I dated Eric for seven months and after getting permission from his commanding officer he proposed to me. He was a year younger than I and I almost accepted, but my cousin, Terry Medaris, who was in the Air Force and came to Bangkok on R&R gave me some advice. He told me to wait until I met Eric on home ground so I told Eric I'd rather make that decision when he got home, which was going to be soon."

Patti reflects back on her decision. "I'm glad I listened to Terry because when Eric and I met in New York City, I saw a different side to him. One day I took the two of us to Greenwich, Connecticut. It would have been a nice trip to see all the mansions in that city, but Eric thought we were going to Greenwich Village. Looking back, I can laugh about it now, but he was really irate. Things seemed to have changed between us so I took an early flight back to Decatur, Illinois where I was staying and never heard from him again. It was probably for the best, but he was quite a character and a true patriot who loved 'Tricky Dicky'."

Note:

After David John "Eric" Erickson was shot down and rescued while being a forward air traffic controller (FAC) in Vietnam, he volunteered for an even more dangerous job of flying in support of the clandestine CIA missions in Laos as a Raven FAC and would survive another crash.

The casualty rate for OV-10 Bronco pilots ran about 50% wounded and killed. One calculation by a participating Raven at his end of tour was that 90% of the Raven planes had been hit by ground fire during their tours of duty; 60% had been downed by enemy action at some point; 30% of pilots had been killed in action.

Chapter 11
Pickets, Bikinis and Protests

It was not always a charmed adventure for women flight attendants during the Vietnam War years. In 1970 after a year of failed negotiations, World Airways' flight attendants rebelled against management and went on strike. The dispute included hour and wage demands and triggered picket lines in Japan, Spain, England, Ireland, Holland, Mexico and several U.S. cities. The ladies knew how to grab the spotlight. Accustomed to airport runways, several World flight attendants stripped down to their bikinis and walked their own runway.

Not all flight attendants bared their flesh during the six-week strike. One who kept all her clothes on was Janet Bancroft (Burttram) who had been on furlough for six months before joining the strike.

Janet Bancroft (Burttram) left and unidentified flight attendant at World
Airways maintenance center in Oakland

A telegram Janet received was a cleverly disguised message that
suggested it would be best if she returned to work.

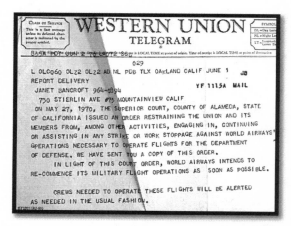

It read, "ON MAY 27, 1970, THE SUPERIOR COURT, COUNTY OF
ALAMEDA, STATE OF CALIFORNIA ISSUED AN ORDER
RESTRAINING THE UNION AND ITS MEMBERS FROM, AMONG
OTHER ACTIVITIES, ENGAGING IN, CONTINUING OR ASSISTING
IN ANY STRIKE OR WORK STOPPAGE AGAINST WORLD
AIRWAYS' OPERATIONS NECESSARY TO OPERATE FLIGHTS FOR

THE DEPARTMENT OF DEFENSE. WE HAVE SENT YOU A COPY OF THIS ORDER.

IN LIGHT OF THIS COURT ORDER, WORLD AIRWAYS INTENDS TO RE-COMMENCE ITS MILITARY FLIGHT OPERATIONS AS SOON AS POSSIBLE.

CREWS NEEDED TO OPERATE THESE FLIGHTS WILL BE ALERTED AS NEEDED IN THE USUAL FASHION.

Picket line in Japan with pilots, flight engineers, navigators and flight attendants, part of Teamsters Local 2707

The Koza Riot

On the night of Sunday December 20, 1970, seven months after the World Airways strike was settled and a thousand miles south of the Tokyo picket lines, a violent and spontaneous protest erupted. It was on the Japanese island of Okinawa in the city of Koza that bordered Kadena Air Force Base.

Although most of Japan regained independence in 1952, Okinawa Prefecture remained under U.S. military occupation for another twenty years. When that turnover date approached, tensions between civilians and the military exploded on December 20 following a minor traffic accident. Things quickly escalated and over the next eight hours 5,000 Okinawans clashed with 700 American MPs. Sixty people were injured, 80 cars were torched and several buildings on the Kadena base were destroyed, including the offices of the *Stars and Stripes* newspaper.

Koza, Japan, March 1970

Koza riot December 1970

Chapter 12
Destination: Home

For the military troops who made it through their tour in Vietnam alive, they weren't just going home, they were returning to the world.

Saigon
Courtesy: BJ Elliott
Behind My Wings

Patti Medaris said the troops would say that Vietnam was hell and America was the world.

Most of the time, the flights were filled with good cheer and no desire to look back, but on Christmas Eve 1967 there was a close call for a Flying Tiger Line 707 filled with troops returning to America. One of the flight attendants on board was Patti.

"We were taking off from Kadena Air Force Base in Okinawa," Patti remembers, "on our way to Anchorage taking a full load of soldiers when we lost two of the four engines. The pilots had to dump fuel over the ocean before returning to Kadena. We told the boys to be quiet and remain in their seats."

It's hard to imagine the thoughts of the troops on board, all having survived their year's tour in the combat zone and thinking now they might be killed while flying home.

"Smoking was forbidden," Patti said, "and ground crews foamed the runway for our return landing as we circled over the ocean to get rid of most of our fuel."

The pilots were able to get the crippled plane safely on the runway. Christmas Eve and Christmas Day were spent in Okinawa while the plane's engines were repaired. On December 26, the Flying Tiger plane, its crew and passengers safely returned to the States.

Janet Bancroft (Burttram) recalled a similar experience on a flight leaving Yokota Air Force Base. "We were heading to Travis AFB and we had a landing gear that would not retract. We needed to dump fuel before returning to base and the emergency lights and equipment were flashing. The guys took it all in stride and said after what they went through this was nothing. We landed safely, the problem was fixed and we made it home."

* * * * *

Continental flight attendant JoAnn Wright (Wintenburg) will never forget a horror trip of another kind that brought her into the teeth of a typhoon in Okinawa.

She said, "We had one trip where we encountered so much turbulence and landed on our fifth approach to Okinawa only because we were out of fuel. The fear of hydroplaning was the danger but all I recall was that everyone including me was airsick on that flight. I had to lay down on the floor and remained there for landing.

"Things were bouncing around and I knew we were going to die and just wanted to get it over with. I was so sick! I only knew of two passengers that did not vomit on that flight out of 165 passengers. One of our flight attendants went thru the cabin with a huge trash bag picking up the barf bags and the guys would hold on to her so she would not fall during the turbulence. We eventually ran out of barf bags and the stench in the cabin was unbelievable. Even the second officer got airsick on that unbelievably rough ride. I never heard how the next crew handled the odor in the cabin when they had to take that same plane out a couple of hours later."

* * * * *

All flight attendants have their own horror stories of life and peril at

30,000 feet.

"One Airlift flight I remember coming home to Yokota," Patti Medaris (Culea) says, "we were in a monsoon and I couldn't see how the plane could hold together. We were all over the sky. The pilots told us to strap in and not get up. Did we ever! Fortunately we had seasoned passengers and no one panicked."

And then there was another scare on Flying Tiger Line. "When flying from the U.S. on Tigers," said Patti, "we were told about something called "clear air turbulence." You never knew when it would happen. I remember once we dropped over 1,000 feet. We'd hit the ceiling of the plane and then drop to the floor. The military guys grabbed us and held us tightly to prevent us being injured. Of course, they probably hoped we'd hit clear air turbulence more often so they could 'rescue' us."

* * * * *

During the monsoon season, once their trips were over and they were back on solid ground, there was no guarantee their problems were over when they returned to where they were living.

Patti Medaris (Culea) remembers, "Several times we were told to fill every container we could with water because when the monsoons hit, the water where we lived would be cut off. We'd fill our bathtub, too."

* * * * *

Unlike the flights over to Vietnam when most of the troops flew as units to the combat zone; the trip back home was different.

"Generally speaking, most of the guys on the airplane did not know each other," said Helen Tennant (Hegelheimer), "and didn't serve with each other so they were looking around for somebody they had come over with."

Their common bond was that they had made it out alive.

Cam Ranh Bay
Courtesy: BJ Elliott
Behind My Wings

* * * * *

All flight attendants remembered one thing returning troops could not get enough of after a year in the jungles was fresh milk. Nancy (Wood) Shammel of World Airways will never forget one flight.

"Some of us gals decided to have fun with this one guy who kept asking for milk. We gave him his milk out of a baby bottle from the Baby Kit. He had a great sense of humor and everyone got such a kick out of this that whenever he wanted more milk he had to have it out of the baby bottle."

Nancy (Wood) Shammel
Courtesy World Airways

"These times were good; it was great to know the soldiers on our plane had lived through hell and could laugh and enjoy their flight home."

* * * * *

Flight attendant Leslie Laird (Pfeifer) developed a deep respect for those who served. She saw some return in casts and bandages, others who had lost limbs. She saw men whose suffering was not just physical, coming back to a nation that was largely oblivious.

"I lived in Berkeley during those years," she said. "I'd come home to armbands and protests and people not even knowing the numbers of casualties. Our boys were dying by the thousands. It was such a dichotomy to come home to an ungrateful nation."

Patti Medaris remembers how important it was for troops on her flights to know what the time it was back home. "On the return flights from Vietnam the boys would ask us what time it was in the world (Vietnam was hell, home was the world.) I ended up buying a huge watch that had the world time on it."

Seiko watch similar to the timepiece Patti bought and the
September 30, 1970 receipt from Pontiac Audio Center in Tokyo showing
the purchase for 21,600 yen (60 USD)

"We flew GMT time so it took a lot of brainpower to figure out the
proper time. But with the special watch I could dial to their time zone and
tell them what time it was at their home. Bless their hearts! They were so
glad to have made it on those planes for their trip home."

* * * * *

There were thousands of other soldiers, Marines, sailors and airmen who
came home in a box. Often accompanying them would be designated escorts
for dependents of deceased military members. In 1970 the nickname "Blue
Bark" was used to designate members of the Department of Defense and
their dependents who traveled in connection with the death of a member or
his dependent.

February 9, 1965
Flag-draped coffins of eight American servicemen killed at Pleiku, South
Vietnam. Vietnamese and U.S. medals,
awarded posthumously are pinned on the flags.

Flight attendants working MAC flights would be alerted to give "Blue
Bark" passengers every possible courtesy including expediting their
movement and not having them get off the flight except for a military
emergency. Other ways to make it easier during the difficult time was to
provide nursery facilities and attendants if needed, arrange for a chaplain
and speeding up customs and immigration clearances.

* * * * *

The bodies of many troops killed in action passed through Okinawa that
had some of the military's mortuary services. And there were visual
reminders on the island of battles in Vietnam. A section of Makiminato
Service Area had the nickname "The Bone Yard" because piles of jeeps and
trucks, many covered in blood and bullet holes were sent to Okinawa from
the combat zone for repair.

Kadena Air Base was the Pentagon's key transport hub, compiling a
million flights during the war including B-52's that took off from the base to
bomb Southeast Asia. Okinawa's capital, Naha Port processed three-fourths
of all supplies, including fuel, food and ammunition. About 50,000
Okinawans were on the U.S. military payroll.

* * * * *

World Airways flight attendant Lorna McLearie wrote about what they sometimes had to carry home.

"Often we had flag-draped coffins in the cargo area and if the flight was configured like this we had to go through a mock door to give the cockpit their meals. We always tried to make sure the guys never saw that area and opened the door just enough to get through. These flights were usually on a 727 flight within the Far East and then cargo transferred to a larger aircraft."

And then Lorna recalls the moment of arrival.

"I remember landing at Travis Air Force base at the end of a very long duty day and often the troops clapping would jar our sleepy heads on landing. They had made it home, and you hoped their return was one of peace."

Another trip for Lorna seemed to be a preview of a movie that would be released in 1982.

"We were going to fly an empty airplane into Saigon and take civilians to Bangkok. I remember the pilot was from Australia. Most of our pilots had military backgrounds. We had to do more of a deep descent into the airport because of the risk. We landed in Saigon and boarded passengers as quickly as we could and took off for Bangkok.

"When we arrived in Bangkok I went inside the airport but didn't stay long as it was so hot, noisy and packed with people. I could barely breathe with the heat. Years later it would remind me of the 1982 movie 'The Year of Living Dangerously.' I had been in the airport many times before to pick up fresh pineapple for the flight crew. But on that day everything was very different and unsettling.

"We then returned to Saigon and picked up civilians who were nervous and eager to get out of the country. You could hear a pin drop on the airplane before we left.

"I remember standing on the jet-way outside the aft cabin door and a man approached me and said, 'How much longer?' I felt his urgency to get out and realized then the risk we were involved in.

"I still felt calm and remember telling him we would be leaving soon, trying to ease his fear. When we took off there was a silence in the cabin we were not used to.

"In later years I reflected on these many flights into Saigon, Da Nang and am sure it was my youth that gave me confidence that everything would be OK.

"On some military flights the troops were frightened and upset that we were not ordering people to turn off overhead lights because they were used to flying in darkness. The overhead lights had not been an issue for guys going over, because they had not known or experienced the war yet, only the pain of leaving loved ones.

"With so many military flights, if I allowed myself I would have been overwhelmed with the passenger's sadness of leaving loved ones. They would attach family photos to their meal tray lock so they could stare at them on the long flights."

As for her final flight from Vietnam, Lorna McLearie recalls this scene.

"We deadheaded back to the states into San Francisco airport," she said. "We were standing waiting for our crew bus. As I was alongside other flight attendants, a taxi cab driver approached me. He said, 'I know you don't remember me, as there were so many of us, but I will never forget you, as you were on my trip out of Vietnam.' In that moment I felt peace. I told him I was glad I had worked his trip out and that he was safely home. We wished each other well and hugged goodbye. The crew bus appeared with the World Airways logo, which probably confirmed to him who I was but the timing of being there was no accident."

* * * * *

It wasn't just the flight attendants who wondered how many of the troops they brought in would not be coming home alive.

Former combat Marine Corps veteran Conrad Lopez, writing on an online forum tells of waiting to board a Pan Am flight to Okinawa.

"One thing that always stuck in my memory," he writes, "was standing on the tarmac watching my flight out deplane fresh troops who were replacing us and wondering how many of them would not make it home.

"I was a combat grunt, got shot twice, had a pretty full experience there in 67–68 and I have to tell you, most of the time it would have made for a pretty boring movie. I'm pretty sure that is true of all "war movies" ever made."

* * * * *

Patti Medaris (Culea) recalls the troops on return flights.

"Those coming home were different," she says. "We couldn't have enough milk on board as we went through gallons from Vietnam to Okinawa or Japan and then again from Okinawa to Travis, or wherever. They were quiet, not wanting any kisses, but when the wheels went up leaving Vietnam, they cheered and when we touched down in the States they cheered. They'd get off the plane in Travis or El Toro and kiss the ground. Then reality hit. Outside many of the bases were the draft dodgers, the communists and the haters of these amazing young people. It was an awful time."

* * * * *

Flying Tiger Line flight attendant Leslie Laird (Pfeifer) remembered the troops cheering when the flight landed in the U.S. Some were in casts and bandages and others had lost limbs but their service and sacrifices were largely ignored.

"I lived in Berkeley during those years," she said. "I'd come home to armbands and protests and people not even knowing the numbers of casualties. Our boys were dying by the thousands. It was such a dichotomy to come home to an ungrateful nation."

* * * * *

Bravery was not confined to the battlefield. World Airways flight attendant Janet Bancroft (Burttram) will never forget one flight returning to the states. It began in Vietnam for a flight to Yokota AFB in Japan.

"I was serving coffee to a guy by the window," she says. "They had to put their coffee cup on our small tray that I extended to him. As he put the cup on my tray, blood dripped onto the tray. He looked very sheepish. It turns out he was wounded that morning and he didn't tell anyone because it would have meant he couldn't travel that day if they found out. They would have held him back so he made sure that didn't happen."

* * * * *

Flight attendant Helen Tennant (Hegelheimer) has mixed memories of flights returning troops home.

"We took 19, 20-year-old troops to Vietnam," she says. "When they came home, we knew they were only a year older; we really did know it, but we couldn't tell. So much so, that we had a game going on--let's see if we can guess this soldier or Marine's age. The war was written all over their faces. They were quiet. They acted a little bit strange. They had what is now called PTSD (Post Traumatic Stress Disorder) but we didn't have a name for it back then."

Helen says there were always troops on board who got the nickname "galley bums" because they wanted to hang out in the back of the plane and talk non-stop with the flight attendants.

"I've heard stories about guys cheering when the plane took off from Vietnam," she says, "but I don't remember any cheering; it was quiet. Pretty soon the captain came on and said, 'Gentlemen, we have just cleared Vietnam airspace.' It still gets to me; it was as if everyone on the plane exhaled. But they still didn't cheer.

"On the way back we walked down the aisle looking to see which ones might want to talk and which ones you ought to leave alone. You'd just start by asking, 'Where are you from?' I clearly remember thinking these guys are not going home to their girlfriends and that '55 Chevy they had been working on. Their youth was gone, and it showed. You absolutely saw a different look in their eyes on the way home. There were guys who came up to me and said, 'I need to talk because I want to practice. I'm afraid I'm going to swear in front of my mother when I get home.'

"These boys grew up the same way I did in the 50's. We attended church; we knew right from wrong I believe.

"Flying in, some guys asked, 'How bad are the anti-war demonstrations?' That's the hardest question I've had to answer in my life. I'd say, 'they're bad.' There were often protesters at the gates outside Travis. I had to tell these guys that had just served their country to get out of their country's uniform as soon as they could. If they weren't wearing their uniform then maybe they wouldn't be targeted by the protesters. I didn't like the antiwar movement then and I haven't changed my mind today. They came home so quickly; they had no time to adjust. Some men had just gotten out of combat a few hours before they got on the plane. Before meal service, we'd make sure everyone was awake. We had to be very careful about waking these guys up. If you touched them they'd wake up defending themselves— arms flying all over the place. We managed to hold them until they realized where they were. It only took a second and we always smiled. They always apologized. 'Oh ma'am, I'm sorry, I didn't hurt you did I?' We'd try not to make a big deal out of it."

A big deal was the first sight of home.

"It seems to me we hit the California coast during the day time. It was always on the left side that the California coast would come up first and the captain would announce, 'Hey, guys, that's the California coast line, there's the world.' They just all spilled over to one side of the airplane to take one look at it and a little bit of laughter and normalness entered the airplane.

"Every time we arrived at Travis I was disappointed. I had grown up with WWII movies and everybody had a band or something to welcome them home. At Travis there was absolutely nothing. It was just me at the bottom of the ramp. An ungrateful nation let some 23-year-old stewardess welcome these guys home. That was their only greeting."

To this day, Helen prefers using the term "welcome home" when it comes to Vietnam veterans and thinks "thank you for your service" has been overused.

"The Vietnam Vet did not get the 'welcome home' they should have," she said.

* * * * *

Vietnam veteran and Army Specialist 4 (E-4) Bob Hirsch was with the famed 101st Airborne, 2nd Battalion, 506th Infantry Regiment.

The native Hoosier now 70 and living in San Diego, California arrived in Vietnam on his 21st birthday and was in the combat zone 16 months from 1970 to 1971. He tells what happened at the end of his tour of duty on his way home.

Bob Hirsch (1970 and 2019)

"I flew Continental Airlines back to the U.S.," he remembers. "We landed at McChord Air Force Base in Washington. The flight was quiet with very little talk or laughing, much different than when we flew to Vietnam. As soon as we got off the plane we were directed to a long line of guys who were being processed for discharge. The wait was unbelievable and the line hardly moved. I ended up sleeping in line for 30-hours. There was a lot of grumbling and things got tense when we would see officers being able to go to the front of the line.

"Things changed when one officer went to the front and asked how long we had been waiting. When he was told, he went to the back of the line and got a huge ovation."

* * * * *

After spending one year in combat, Jim Sellers flew home September 5, 1968 on Flying Tiger Line. The days leading up to his departure were filled with a sense of foreboding.

Jim Sellers 1968

"I was not just grateful to be leaving," he remembers, "but my sense of dread and paranoia seemed to increase. After a year of mortar, rocket and small arms fire . . . and after seeing fellow soldiers die randomly and others survive for no apparent reason, a sense of impending doom permeated my thoughts and feelings."

Jim had heard stories of soldiers who were killed in route to their departure or while being debriefed at a processing center or dying in a rocket attack while waiting at the airport for their flight home.

"I left Vietnam from Ben Hoa airbase (25 miles northeast of Saigon)," he says. "I remember clearly when our Flying Tiger aircraft pulled up and parked on the tarmac adjacent to the terminal. The jet seemed larger than other commercial jets I had flown on. I found out later that it was a stretched DC-8. The Flying Tiger version could carry 260 passengers.

"As the fresh soldiers deplaned it seemed that the plane would never empty. I watched these new arrivals closely and felt sad for what they were about to experience.

"It was a typical hot and humid day. The plane had air conditioning, but it did not operate without the engines running. . . I sat in one of the last rows of the plane and noticed there were no compartments and no bulkheads. From the back of the plane it seemed like an impossibly long tube."

Even though Jim had endured months in the stifling jungles he was surprised by the heat and humidity inside the plane.

"Everyone of us began to sweat profusely. There was no ground power at

Ben Hoa and after some time sitting on a tropical tarmac the plane turned into a first-class sauna."

It was then he took particular notice of the flight attendants.

"I was taken aback by the stewardesses," he says. "Like all soldiers . . . after a year away from my own culture, looking face-to-face with an attractive woman fresh from home was certainly pleasurable but somehow unsettling. Unfortunately, the stewardesses were just as affected by the heat and humidity as we were. We were sitting in our seats and they were working. Their perfectly applied makeup began to run down their faces as they attempted to get us ready for take-off.

"When the engines started and we began to taxi, the air conditioning gave us hope that our sauna was ending. . . Once in the air the temperature inside the plane must have dropped 30 or 40 degrees. Very quickly we were uncomfortably cold, shivering because our uniforms were soaked. Every soldier on that flight was clamoring for a blanket. The stewardesses were rushing back and forth trying to accommodate us. Within thirty minutes we were dry and comfortable again and we wanted the stewardesses to take the blankets back. The Flying Tiger flight attendants did all this without complaint. They served us two meals on the long flight home and treated us with kindness we had almost forgotten existed."

* * * * *

What began as an exciting adventure with Flying Tiger Line for Patti Medaris (Culea) ended with disappointment and disillusion.

"In April 1968 the head flight attendant at Tigers called me into her office in Los Angeles," Patti remembers, "and told me that someone had seen me in uniform having an alcoholic drink on a PSA flight from LAX to San Francisco and that I was fired. I remembered there was a delay on that flight and PSA gave out complimentary drinks. I accepted a drink but it was just a Coke."

At that point, the mental impact on Patti flying troops into combat knowing many would not return alive was becoming more difficult to live with.

"It was getting too hard seeing so many boys going to their deaths," she said. "So, I did not contest the drinking charge. I handed over my identification card, walked out and not long after that I bought a one-way plane ticket to Maui, Hawaii. I arrived with $45 to my name and it was there that I vegged for several months."

Finding a job in Hawaii was a challenge.

"The locals were suspicious of newcomers and wouldn't consider you for a job unless you had lived on the islands for at least six months," she said. "They thought I was a hippie because at that time they were coming to the islands by the thousands."

While some people were distrustful, there was one occasion when Patti saw the opposite.

"I was walking to a hotel about three miles away on Kaanapali," she said, "when I walked by a house. The guy who lived there, I think his last name was McQueen, was working in his garden and asked me where I was going. I told him I was going to try to get a job at the Kaanapali Beach Hotel. He said, 'that's a long walk, why don't you use my car.' It was a dune buggy and I said to him, 'you don't even know who I am.' And his reply was, 'This is a small island, where do you think you're going to take it (the car).'"

As it turned out, Patti got a job working as a first mate on a fishing boat out of Lahaina in Maui that was docked near the Pioneer Inn where she first stayed.

The Pioneer Inn and Patti on the dock

"After that I went to Whidbey Island in Washington, then to Aspen,

Colorado, Bement, Illinois and back to Phoenix, Arizona," she said.

But, being a flight attendant was still in her blood. About a year and a half after leaving Tigers, she wanted to get back in the air.

"September 1969 I got a call from Jackie Lange, one of the gals I used to work with at Tigers," Patti said. "She told me that Airlift International (a CIA-backed airline) was looking for any experienced flight attendants to live in Japan. I jumped at that. I was working at a travel agency in Phoenix and the manager, Jeannie Moore encouraged me to apply. I remember calling and they already had my name down because Jackie or another flight attendant I worked with Robin Burkey had told them they'd talked with me. I did not go for an interview; they hired me over the phone. I gave Jeannie two weeks' notice and I was gone."

Patti began with Airlift on October 1, 1969 and because she already had been through training with Flying Tigers her training session was only two weeks.

"They were desperate for flight attendants," she said.

"We then flew in and out of Travis AFB in California on stretch DC-8's through Anchorage, Alaska. We didn't fly that often to Kadena; mostly to Yokota AFB near Tokyo. We stayed at the Hotel Momiyama in Tachikawa. Tachikawa Air Base had closed and all MAC flights were in and out of Yokota, but the contracts for the hotels were still in Tachikawa,"

Around February 1970 four of us flight attendants lived in a two bedroom, one bath home in Fussa near Yokota Air Force Base. The house was owned by an American who rented it to crew members," Patti said. "The western-style bathroom was disappointing. I wanted it to be

Japanese. We slept on the floor on futons, all very basic."

"Nearby was a crematorium and it was a bit spooky because sometimes the ashes would settle on our house. No smell that I can remember."

The silk painting of a horse on the wall was bought in Taipei.

"We had to purchase a black market phone since getting regular phone service was a six-month wait. No mobile phones in those days, and because we'd be on call often we had to have a phone. One of my roommates arranged the phone through an Airlift pilot who had an inside contact. We paid a small monthly fee since we rarely called out.

"Across the street from us was a very nice home, much larger than normal in Japan," she said. "The Japanese owner and his wife would have us over for dinner, but only one at a time. This helped us learn Japanese. We picked up enough of the language to be able to buy groceries and other necessary items. When we had problems with plumbing or the water heater we'd contact the landlord. The water heater was another story.

"We were told that if no one was going to be home for 24 hours to turn off the water heater. If it weren't turned off, it would build up pressure and the top would blow off. That happened once and fortunately I wasn't the first one to come home. They found the top two blocks away. After that we made sure that never happened again."

One of Patti's roommates

The months in Japan bring vivid memories for Patti.

"Ray Charles and Lou Rawls came to the officer's club at Yokota," Patti says.

She learned that Ray Charles would have someone walk him from his dressing area to the stage and then to the piano.

"He memorized the steps," she marveled. "When he was introduced he would walk out unaided and go directly to the piano and sit down and start playing and singing. Amazing."

The officer's club was also where she got the best French onion soup she ever had. But she shakes her head and continues. "It was also a place when things got rather rowdy. One evening we all met at the officer's club at Yokota when Eric (John "Eric" Erickson, mentioned earlier in the book) had proposed to me. When the wine steward brought the wine for my roommate to taste, she stunned the poor waiter by gargling the wine."

It seems that Patti was the most accomplished player of something called "Liar's Dice," a game at a bar using several pairs of di and players who call out what they have, but sometimes lying to avoid having to buy a round of drinks.

"I usually won because I guess I looked like some innocent girl who could never tell a lie," she says.

And then there were the so-called "carrier landings" at the officer's club bar.

"Basically, it involved less-than-sober pilots," Patti explained. "They would put tables together and wet them with beer. They would then take a running jump and slide on the table. Two guys were holding ropes and the object for the person sliding was to try to catch the rope and hook it with their ankle, before they slid off the end of the table."

Did anyone get hurt?

"Are you kidding. They were too drunk," Patti says with a chuckle.

After a night like that it is no wonder that Patti enjoyed going to a place everyone called "Kay's Happy Landing."

"After long flights, we'd go to Kay's that was within walking distance of our house. Kay's was a bath and massage house. No sex, nothing seedy but for $2.50 we'd get a bath, massage and sushi and sake. It was heaven and when it was over, we'd be like jelly and have to take a taxi back to our house."

* * * * *

"When we had enough days off in a row we'd visit other parts of Japan within 50 miles of our base. We spent a lot of time in Tokyo. We'd take the train, which was close to our house. That was when I first saw professional packers who jammed people into trains and subways during rush hour. Once was enough and we tried to avoid rush hour. The Ginza District was a favorite for eating at the noodle shops and having sushi. But, we didn't eat in the Ginza that often since it was a lot more expensive than Fussa.

"We didn't have commissary privileges, but we could go to the Air Force Base Exchange although, while living in Fussa we shopped locally as much as we could.

"Recycling in the town of Fussa was important. The Japanese had various carts that had several bells. The different bells would let you know which cart was coming to receive specific recycled material. You would then exchange your empty cans for filled cans (canned vegetables, fruit, etc.); the same was true for paper goods; mainly exchanging toilet paper rolls for full rolls of TP. There were recycling bins in every neighborhood and we were encouraged to use them. No garbage trucks came rumbling down the narrow streets."

* * * * *

Little did Patti know that her airline adventure was about to have a royal chapter.

"While I was flying for Airlift," Patti recalls, "Through a friend, Al Blomberg, I met Chai, a member of the Thai royal family in Bangkok.

Chai

"Al had gone to college in Indiana with Chai and they remained good friends. Chai arranged a meeting for me with King Bhumibol Adulyadej and his wife, Queen Siriki at the palace.

The Amarin Winichai Throne Hall, Grand Palace, Bangkok, Thailand
Photo courtesy: Sodacan

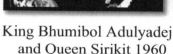

King Bhumibol Adulyadej   Queen Sirikit
and Queen Sirikit 1960   1962

"Chai and I were escorted into a small room that had spectacular gold leaf on all the walls. I had wondered if the king and queen would be seated on thrones and was relieved to see them on cushioned chairs.

"Chai bowed and since I had been instructed on how to greet them, I also bowed. We then sat in chairs across from the king and queen with a beautiful carved teak table between us for an informal tea. Men dressed in black and white silk then entered the room with tea and pastries.

"Both the king and queen spoke perfect English and were charming. They had been educated in America and England before finishing in Switzerland when they were married and their first daughter was born there. He was named King while in Switzerland after his brother passed away in Bangkok.

"I remember them asking me about my childhood and Chai told them that he had lived in Indiana next to the state where I grew up. It was not a long event; I think only about 30 minutes since there were many meetings scheduled for the king. Or, maybe it was just a courtesy towards Chai. I only remember how excited I was and how humbling it was to meet such distinguished people. I also remember my roommates were quite impressed.

"In the weeks to come I made several visits to the palace to see Chai. I stayed at the Siam Intercontinental Hotel and Chai would come with a limousine to pick me up.

Siam Intercontinental Hotel
Before 2002 demolition

"I can still see the faces of people outside the hotel," Patti says with a laugh. "When the big black limo with royal flags on it would pull up to the hotel the driver and an aide would get out to open the door and greet me. Chai remained in the car and I could see people near the hotel's front entrance looking in amazement at each other wondering who I was."

What about any romance between the American beauty and the Thai prince? Perhaps a different version of *"The King and I"*?
"There was only friendship," Patti says with a smile. "I think he took a liking to me because I was short. Much different than most American girls who towered over him."

* * * * *

Patti saw first-hand the wide disparity between the social elite and most of the Thai people. Looking out the limousine windows the contrast of what she saw and where she was going was stark.

Roadside peasants in Bangkok

"The King and Queen loved the people as did Chai," Patti says, "and while they tried to be kind and compassionate, the socio-economic gulf between classes in Thailand will always be great. But even so, I never saw so many happy people, even those who lived along the river. I learned quickly why it is called 'The Land of Smiles.'"

* * * * *

Patti's time in Thailand and Japan was largely positive but there was one moment following an international faux pas when Patti had to make right with the Emperor of Japan.

"While I was with Airlift, I had to write a letter of apology to the Emperor of Japan. It happened after I had a chance to jump on a *Stars & Stripes* flight (a plane that was carrying the *Stars & Stripes* newspaper) to Bangkok to meet up with Eric. I forgot to get my passport stamped when I left Japan. When I arrived back in Japan they noticed I didn't have a departure stamp. Very serious. I could have been arrested and placed in jail but the officer said that I should write a letter of apology to the Emperor. I did and they contacted Airlift to let me know I was pardoned."

* * * * *

In late 1970 Patti's magical stay in the Far East was about to end when she learned that Airlift was planning wide spread furloughs.

"When I found out I was going stateside Chai offered me a job teaching English to children at a school at the Royal Palace," she says, "but I felt it wasn't for me."

Still wanting to fly she went to Taipei looking for a job.

"A couple of us interviewed with Air America in Taipei. I didn't get hired, as I was too short. Tighter standards than Airlift, I guess. But I think when we were told we were going home we were all ready. I loved Japan, but we were all craving a good, juicy hamburger and fries. When we got back to Oakland we did a couple of trips to Yokota and Vietnam, but I think it was by mid-November that we were officially furloughed.

"Airlift's contract was up, and we had to go to the U.S. Embassy in Tokyo for our pay. We went a couple weeks with no paycheck, but eventually got paid.

"October 1970 was when we flew back to Oakland from Japan. We went back and forth to Vietnam until the end of November and then we were all furloughed. Because I knew we would not be flying that much longer after we got back to Oakland, I had everything packed in Japan and shipped to Grandma LeFever in Illinois. We didn't have a lot as the house we rented was furnished and I remember leaving a couple of lamps and some pots and pans we'd purchased for the house there."

* * * * *

Patti's household effects in Fussa packed and ready to go

Patti's flight home on Airlift had the guy on the left looking through binoculars, which seemed symbolic of the CIA-operated airline.

Chapter 13
The Sounds of the Times

Our senses bring instant, intense memories and for men and women who lived through life-changing events during the Vietnam War years, sometimes only a song or a picture will make today seem like yesterday.

The music of that era was a constant companion for soldiers, Marines, sailors, airmen and the women flight attendants who flew with the troops to war. And for those men who survived, they came back home with sounds that would always connect with the past.

While in the combat zone, troops listened to music in the bush and in bunkers. Sony radios and Akai stereos were easily available and priced cheap at the base exchanges.

Some troops believe music got them through Vietnam while others today, including flight attendants find the songs can help heal painful emotions that are still raw.

Former World Airways flight attendant Fredene Weaver (Maulhardt) had one of those moments in February 2019.

"Listening to Pandora tonight," she writes, "John Denver's 'Take Me Home, Country Roads,' came on and it sparked a vivid memory of bringing soldiers from Vietnam and a fellow playing the guitar singing that song. I sensed his gratefulness to be alive and coming home."

John Denver 1975

Music of previous wars was used to instill patriotism and purpose during those times. Song's like George M. Cohan's 1917 "Over There," propelled troops to battle with courage yet little knowledge of the horrors that awaited them in the trenches.

Two decades later, Vera Lynn's 1939 "We'll Meet Again" resonated with troops going off to war promising what proved to be a less-than-certain guarantee of coming home to families and sweethearts.

The Vietnam War years had a few songs with positive intentions such as Barry Sadler's "Ballad of the Green Beret's."

It was written and sung by Army Staff Sergeant Barry Sadler at the start of his training to be a Special Forces medic. The lyrics, in part honored U.S. Army Specialist 5 James Gabriel Jr., a Special Forces operator killed by Viet Cong gunfire while with the South Vietnamese Army on April 8, 1962.

* * * * *

Merle Haggard struck a sympathetic chord for conservatives with the song "Okie from Muskogee" that spoke of not taking drugs or burning draft cards and waving the American flag.

Merle Haggard 1971

The majority of music, however, reflected questions about the war by those fighting the battles in jungles or protesting back home. Echoing those feelings were such songs as "Fortunate Son" by Creedence, Clearwater Revival.

Creedence, Clearwater Revival

John Fogerty wrote the song in 20 minutes that has been a classic for a half century. His lyrics supported those who felt young men in privileged positions were given a deferment or able to avoid combat in the war.

Another song with a clear statement was 'We Gotta Get Out of This Place" by Eric Burdon and The Animals. Forgotten for the most part are the verses leading up to the chorus that was repeated by our troops at the top of their lungs over and over in the field and in clubs that "We Gotta Get Out of

This Place!"

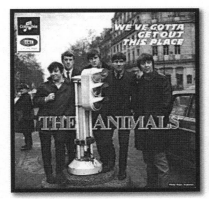

Then there were The Box Tops who went top of the charts in 1967 with "The Letter," a song by Alex Chilton that troops in anticipation of flying home sang, "Give me a ticket for an aeroplane."

A different kind of homecoming may be suggested in the Rolling Stones 1966 song "Paint It Black."

Some believe the song is a picture of a funeral with a line of cars that are all painted black and the unexpected loss of a loved one from the Vietnam War.

Additional Vietnam War-era songs:

"These Boots Were Made for Walking," 1966. Many soldiers picked up Nancy Sinatra's song as their theme.

"Chain of Fools," 1967. When recorded it was not intended to be a Vietnam War protest song but Aretha Franklin's song was embraced by those critical of the military chain of command.

"Purple Haze," 1967. Whether or not the Jimi Hendrix song referred to a drug-induced experience, it was linked to hand grenades that had purple smoke. Three years after the songs release, Hendrix was found dead in a London apartment at age 27.

"Green, Green Grass of Home" 1965 and 1967. Originally about a prisoner longing to return home, the song by Porter Wagoner and Tom Jones resonated with troops in the jungle and at sea who longed to leave Vietnam.

"Sittin on the Dock of the Bay," 1967 reflected loneliness and isolation for troops during the Vietnam War. It was recorded shortly before Otis Redding was killed in a plane crash at age 26.

"Leaving on a Jet Plane"
Written by John Denver 1966 but recorded as a hit by Peter, Paul and Mary in 1969. Everyone wanted to get home from the war.

Photo Courtesy: WBUR

"Whiter Shade of Pale," 1967. The Procol Harum song has nothing to do with the Vietnam War but its haunting melody and Bach-inspired organ background instantly transports us to the late 1960's. Just as a meaning for the Vietnam War had more questions than answers, so it is with trying to explain the lyrics to this song that included "feeling kinda seasick but the crowd called out for more" and "would not let her be one of sixteen vestal virgins."

The song was recorded in just two takes and the lyrics are probably best left unanalyzed

"Riders on the Storm," 1971. This is another memory jogger that has no direct reference to the Vietnam War but the song by The Doors seems a chilling backdrop to the violence that rained down from above and the bloody fighting that was waged on the ground. The single was released shortly before singer Jim Morrison was found dead in a Paris apartment bathtub at age 27.

Jim Morrison

* * * * *

Former flight attendant Janet (Bancroft) Burttram listed "Leaving on a Jet Plane" as a song that beckoned her mind back to Vietnam. Another was the song "Sounds of Silence" by Simon and Garfunkel.

There were chances for Janet and her fellow flight attendants to see and hear musical stars who came to the Far East.

"I was fortunate to be in Okinawa in December of 1970," she writes. "Ike and Tina Turner were doing a USO tour and were performing at the Kadena

Officer's Club. They could really knock 'Proud Mary' out of the park!"

Ike and Tina Turner
1974
* * * * *

Filipino rock bands performed American and English music live, AFVN Radio was heard round the clock and new troops arrived weekly with the latest records from the states. GI-operated underground radio stations, playing mostly hard acid rock, were also part of the in-country counterculture of the war.

* * * * *

Beside vinyl discs, 8-track tapes and transistor radios; a popular way to preserve and listen to music of the day was on large reel-to-reel magnetic tape decks.

One of the most popular brands was TEAC.

The author's TEAC tape deck 1968

A seven-inch reel contained enough quarter-inch tape for about an hour's worth of music.

* * * * *

It did not have to be music to imbed permanent memories of that era. Former flight attendant Patti Medaris (Culea) was mesmerized by the sounds of jet engines.

"When I was with Airlift I used to take a small tape recorder with me and record landings and takeoffs as I sat in the back of the 727," she said. "I was surrounded by the three engines and loved the sounds they made. As a wanna-be fighter pilot, I would say, 'This is landing at Da Nang or Tan Son Nhut (Saigon), etc.'"

Da Nang and Da Nang Air Base

* * * * *

Former flight attendant Janet Bancroft (Burttram) still remembers what she heard at Tan Son Nhut.

"The sounds of Saigon airport were always LOUD," Janet writes, "with jet fighters taking off and landing and also the commercial MAC flights. The revving engines felt like they vibrated inside you. There were no jet-ways there. The aircraft was parked out on the tarmac quite a way from the terminal area, which wasn't very big."

Tan Son Nhut Airport, Saigon

"The airmen rolled out stairways, one for the front door of the jet and one for the aft door. We had flight attendants greeting the soldiers at the bottom of the stairs and others at the top when they entered the plane. When you were at the bottom of the stairs the noise could really get to you. But it was exciting at the same time and I don't think anyone who was in Vietnam during the war will ever forget the noise of the helicopter blades thumping."

UH-1D 1966

For flight attendants, layovers in Japan meant hotel stays and Janet

Bancroft (Burttram) still remembers what she heard at one particular hotel located in the western part of Tokyo.

"The hotel in Fussa was ten feet from a very active train track to and from Tokyo. It might have been even closer. You can imagine the first, startled reaction after a long, tiring flight to settle down for some deserved sleep only to be frightened by a thunderous, passing train. After a while we got used to it and slept through the noise."

But, it was not all bad.

"They had a small restaurant at the hotel," Janet recalls, "and they made the best fried rice in the world. I think a plateful of rice ensured a deep sleep despite the trains!"

Chapter 14
The Sights of the Time

   The mid 1960's and early 1970's were years of enormous change not only in what people heard but what they wore.

   The so-called "English invasion" and the hippie movement brought about mini and micro skirts, skinny ties, ruffled shirts, Nehru jackets, bell bottom pants, John Lennon-type round wire-rim glasses, polyester everything, white belts, tie-dye tops, flowing scarves and above all, the brightest of colors in yellow, orange, blue, pink, red, purple and green.

The author in 1968 while
in the Navy wearing a
skinny tie in front of his bedsitter
apartment 90 Park Street,
London, England

Janet Bancroft (Burttram)
Wearing bell bottoms in Saigon 1969

From head to toe, it included headbands, white suits, platform shoes, long-collared shirts, corduroys, black leather vests, aviator sunglasses, high-rise waistcoats, big buckles, woven belts, strings of gold necklaces, pantsuits, oversized collars, bows, hip huggers, Capri pants, knee-high boots, wide-brimmed hats and super-tight skirts.

Rock groups like The Beatles, The Rolling Stones, Diana Ross and the Supremes, Elvis Presley and Cher influenced how young people dressed.

JoAnn Wright (Wintenburg) (left) shopping in the Philippines 1971

In nearly all the Far East, shopping was done with dollars converted to local currency; however, Patti Medaris (Culea) and others remember having to use Military Payment Certificates (MPCs) in South Korea.

One-dollar bill MPC Series 692, Vietnam War era (1970-73)

MPC's were used to reduce profiteering from currency manipulation, protect the local currency and discourage black markets where U.S. servicemen found a more favorable exchange rate.

The author, while stationed with Commander Naval Forces, Korea was unable to get a U.S. Navy foul-weather jacket through official channels, so when he was a LTJG, he had his name and U.S. Navy sewn on the front and bought one on the black market in Seoul for $25 MPC.

The author at home in his 53-year-old Navy jacket

Chapter 15
Odds and Ends

What follows are selected vignettes, not long enough to merit a separate chapter but part of the story.

From Janet Bancroft (Burttram):
"While we were in Saigon we were warned to keep a tight hold on our purses. They had what was known as 'cowboys' who would drive by on their scooter and cut the strap of your bag while you were holding it and then steal it."

From Patti Medaris (Culea):
"We used to get massages at the Oasis Hotel in the Philippines. They charged $1. You called the front desk and two girls came up. The men on our flights who put their money in their socks, sometimes discovered the soles of the socks were cut away and the money was gone."

* * * * *

"We had been warned that people in the Philippines were corrupt but I found it just the opposite. I always felt safe and never had anything taken. In Angelo City near Clarke Air Force Base we got to know the mayor who hosted parties for us. The van that picked us up at the airport always had a big bucket of San Miguel beer.

"When I was based in Japan with Airlift, we couldn't get good panty hose, but in this place the black market was where we stocked up on all things American including Avon products."

* * * * *

Patti remembered seeing a Kentucky Fried Chicken restaurant through a window across the street from the Oasis Hotel.

"We could hear cockroaches marching across the ceiling and floor," she said, "and occasionally a rat would waltz into our room."

* * * * *

Most flight attendants could tell what branch of the military service their pilots served in by how the planes were brought in for a landing.

"Pilots who were Naval aviators usually brought the plane in harder than the Air Force pilots," said Patti Medaris (Culea). "Especially the 727 that would land like a fighter jet. The stretch 8 did not do a tail down landing."

* * * * *

On January 23, 1968, the USS Pueblo, with a crew of 83, was attacked and captured by North Korea. Commander Lloyd "Pete" commanded the ship and was conducting surveillance of Soviet naval operations. North Korea claimed the ship was in its territorial waters; the United States said *Pueblo* was in international waters. One sailor was killed during the take-over.

USS Pueblo
AGER-2

On the same day Pueblo was captured, Patti Medaris (Culea) was on an Airlift International flight from Da Nang and arrived in Kadena Air Force Base. The plane and crew were immediately grounded because of the Pueblo capture. For two days, Patti and the crew could not leave the base and stayed at the Bachelor Officer's Quarters and hung out at the officer's club.

"Everyone was up-tight as the whole area was on Red Alert (the highest state of alert in which an enemy attack is expected)," she said.

Eleven months after being captured and tortured, Pete Bucher and his crew walked across a bridge in North Korea to freedom.

Commander Lloyd "Pete" Bucher

* * * * *

Patti adds a footnote to the story. "The day before the Pueblo was captured, a wonderful man I met two years earlier at a big banquet for surfers in Huntington Beach passed away. He was Duke Kahanamoku, known around the world as a surfing legend. He died of a heart attack at age 77. I had hoped to go to his funeral but because of the Pueblo incident and security lockdown at Kadena Air Base we couldn't leave the base."

Duke "The Big Kahuna" Kahnamouku
1924

* * * * *

On April 23, 1973, World Airways senior flight attendant Jeannie Wagers (Wiseman) was part of a mandated demonstration for the Federal Aviation Administration (FAA) that their new Boeing 747 when fully loaded with passengers could be safely evacuated in 90 seconds.

U.S. regulations stipulate that a simulated evacuation of aircraft that can seat more than 44 passengers must be conducted within 90 seconds under specified conditions.

Using only five of the 11 exits, the World Airways crew of 13 that included flight attendant Janet Bancroft (Burttram) helped 461 passengers out of the plane.

The demonstration was at Boeing's field in Everett, Washington.

"On the way to the airport," said Jeannie, "I stopped and ordered a case of champagne for the crew since our confidence level was high and I wanted to treat the crew to something extra special after the demonstration."

With World Airways owner Ed Daly plus Boeing, FAA, Northwest and Pan American representatives watching, the signal to evacuate was given and the extraction began. The "passengers" included many people from church groups who were paid $10 a head to participate.

Jeannie Wagers (Wiseman) remembers using a bit more than encouragement to get some people to leave the aircraft. "I had to kick one old guy in the back to go down the slide," she said.

When the drill was over the stopwatch showed 90 seconds and World Airways would receive the highest praise for proficiency, efficiency and good judgment during the test. Only a few people suffered minor abrasions.

"According to the Boeing Company," said Jeannie, "of airlines, World Airways was the only carrier to complete the test successfully the first time."

* * * * *

One reason the crew did so well was that they were thoroughly familiar with the aircraft having been part of the original training procedures for World's 747's. "When we got the 747's, they threw about ten of us in a room and said, 'write up the duties for the bird.'"

* * * * *

In 1971, the White House ordered all servicemen to subject themselves to urinalysis before boarding planes back to the United States. If a serviceman failed to pass his drug test, he was required to stay in country for detoxification. When tested clean, he could then be released back to the U.S.

But sometimes intervention was needed at 30,000 feet for those who wanted to feel even higher.

Janet Bancroft (Burttram) recalls soldiers making a run on the airplane's medical kits and asking for Vick's nose inhalers.

"They would break them and put the Vick's soaked swabs under their tongues for a high. Drugs became more prevalent toward the end. We figured out what was going on and stopped handing them out."

* * * * *

While most of the flight attendants' time was spent taking care of the needs of military people on board there was at least one occasion when they were able to give news about home to sailors in ships at sea.

"We had a chance to talk with sailors by radio from the plane's cockpit," Patti Medaris (Culea) said, "and one of the things they wanted to know was how short the mini-skirts were back home. When I gave the revealing details, there were hoots, hollers and wolf whistles."

* * * * *

Over the years there has been a shift in terminology about people who care for passengers on commercial airlines. It has ranged from stewards/stewardesses, air host/hostesses, cabin attendants, cabin crew and flight attendants. For Jeannie Wagers (Wiseman) there is a clear choice: "Hostess!" she says emphatically. "These are my guests and I will take care of them."

* * * * *

ABC's short-lived series "Pan Am" brought criticism from former flight attendants, especially the impression they wore their hats, jackets and gloves in the cabin when serving passengers. In reality they had smocks and lower-heeled shoes for those duties.

* * * * *

For Patti Medaris (Culea) and other flight attendants on Flying Tiger

Line, once they switched into their inflight serving attire, they had to contend with a feature on their dresses that was an open temptation for the troops on board.

"Our inflight dress was changed in 1968. It was a short orange dress with a zipper down the front and a large ring at the top of the zipper," she says shaking her head in amazement.

Flying Tiger Line
Inflight dresses 1968

"Whoever designed this outfit had no idea what we were up against on the flights to Vietnam. Some of the darling young men heard we wore tiger striped underwear. As we'd walk down the aisles they would pull on the ring to see what was underneath."

"We learned to use a large safety pin to pin the ring to the top of our dresses so they couldn't pull the ring to see what was underneath. We weren't upset. We just knew they were young, hormonal, and scared. But, we also didn't want to expose our underwear, which, I can assure you was not tiger-striped."

Chapter 16
Where Are They Now?

Patti Medaris (Culea)

Patti's home is in San Diego, California where she lives with her husband, John. They have two daughters, Janet in Lufkin, Texas and Heidi, whose home is outside of Brussels, Belgium. They have seven grandchildren.

Patti and John

Patti is a world-renowned cloth doll artist/teacher/author whose travels have taken her to Europe, Australia and around America. That schedule has been cut down by choice to use her artistic gifts through the ministry of Emmanuel Faith Community Church in Escondido, California.

Patti in Steam Punk mode and one of her dolls

At the 45th Annual Reunion for the Flying Tiger Line Pilots' Association in May 2019 in Long Beach, California, Patti was able to meet two of the women she went through training with in 1967.

Andee Wright (Reingold), Patti and Robin Berkey (Pestarino)

Fredene Weaver (Maulhardt)

Fredene lives with her husband John in San Luis Obispo. John is CEO for San Ysidro Farms, Inc. a major vegetable grower in Central California.

John and Fredene Maulhardt

Fredene and John with their family

In 2013, Fredene and her husband, John went to visit Vietnam. Their stops included Ho Chi Min City (Saigon), Hanoi and Hue.

"We were warmly received," Fredene says. "People were happy to see us and we felt no ill will. I cried because the people were treated so poorly."

Janet Bancroft (Burttram)

George and Janet in 1996 at their Lake Tahoe wedding

Janet and her husband, George moved several times while working and in retirement, going from the Big Easy (New Orleans) to the Big Freezie (Anchorage, Alaska) and many places in between. They are currently settled in Southwest Florida enjoying the sunshine.

Janet enjoys anything related to food and wine, fishing and a good book.

One of her greatest passions is dog rescue and she currently volunteers with the Labrador Retriever Rescue of Florida.

The Burttram's try to take one big trip a year and in May 2019 George and Janet went to Southeast Asia with stops in Cambodia and then Saigon and Da Nang, the first time Janet had returned to Vietnam since her flying years.

"It was with great anticipation that I returned to Saigon (I can't seem to call it Ho Chi Minh City and I noticed while there, most of the locals still call Saigon, Saigon). We were on a small cruise ship which navigated up the Saigon River into the city with a pilot onboard.

"On either side of the river it was amazing to see so much open space with just one cleared lot where someone was building a river front home.

"Of course there is still lots of life up and down the river; with many small fishing boats going about their business.

In Hoi An, a town outside Da Nang.

"We took a shuttle into the city and it dropped us off in front of the Caravelle Hotel and opera house.

Janet Bancroft (Burttram)

"The square still looked pretty much the same as I remembered 50 years ago; it was jammed with vehicles, especially scooters zooming around in a country officially committed to socialism but increasingly pro-capitalist.

"The Caravelle Hotel's inside was beautifully updated and though the 10th floor rooftop bar wasn't open, they let George and I take the elevator to see the place where so many war stories were told and written by journalists.

"It was overwhelming to see that the bar's decor has changed little since the "old days." Memories flooded my mind so much that for at least one Nano-second I couldn't breathe.

Caravelle Hotel
Saigon Rooftop Bar

"The hotel has a gift shop near the bar and among items for sale was a pictorial book covering the Caravelle Hotel's history through the 50's (when it first opened), 60's, and 70's. Because they were just beginning to be known as household names, I never realized that Peter Jennings, Peter Arnett and Morley Safer were amongst the hotel regulars. I only remember meeting Howard Tuckner.

"During our stay I experienced no animosity from the Vietnamese people. They were gracious. While I had no in-depth conversations with locals about the war, I did talk to one of our guides in Cambodia who said a while generation was wiped out by the Khmer Rouge. One young man in his late 30's said he never met his grandparents; they were among those killed.

"I met several cruise passengers who served in the war and were returning to Vietnam as civilians. They had their own reasons for returning but being such a personal thing, no one wanted to share their stores. I understood even more when a friend who was a Marine in Vietnam told me that he and a fellow Marine had no desire to "go back to that place," but when I returned wanted to know what I thought.

"Past memories came alive in open markets from smells; some good (openly cooked food with Asian flavors) and some not so good (unrefrigerated fish, meat, etc.).

"I am grateful to have experienced a small part of my "previous" life with my husband who I didn't know when I was in Vietnam. Having had my curiosity satisfied, I'm glad I went and for Vietnam War American veterans who read this book, please accept my heartfelt thanks for all you did."

* * * * *

George Gewehr

George is retired and lives in Tucson with his wife, Julie. They celebrated 50 years of marriage in June 2020. He is active in their local parish church and also with the Flying Tiger Pilots Association (FTLPA) as its historian. His wish is to see the FTLPA continue and the memory live on.

Although the membership grows smaller with pilots who have "Flown West," the FTLPA remains a tightly-knit group with annual reunions.

George Gewehr emceeing an Open Microphone event and wife Julie at the FTLPA 45th Annual Reunion in May 2019 at Long Beach, California

Leslie Laird (Pfeifer)

Leslie and Dave Pfeifer were married in 1972. They met during her Tiger days when he was in the Navy and was a career Navy dentist. They live in Moraga, California.

Lydia Cowgill (Rossi)

Lydia is an accomplished watercolor artist, graphic designer and board member of the Fallbrook Land Conservancy. She lives in her Fallbrook California home with former Navy officer Jerry Kalman.

Jerry Kalman and Lydia

Helen Tennant (Hegelheimer)

After more than 45 years as a technical writer in Silicon Valley, Helen retired to a small town in northern California where she enjoys her five grandchildren and five great-grandchildren. Every Veterans Day for the past 25 years, she has traveled to Washington DC to be with her "boys" at the Vietnam Memorial.

Jeannie Wagers (Wiseman)

Jeannie, a former World Airways flight attendant lives in San Diego with her husband, retired World Airways pilot John Wiseman.

She still has plastic check-off lists from her flying days and the author has no doubt that after a quick refresher course, she could handle any flight on any airline out of Lindbergh Field.

Tom Luczynski

Brigadier General Tom Luczynski

Tom Luczynski is the officer who met former World Airways flight attendant Janet Bancroft (Burttram) while in Vietnam. He is now a Brigadier General in the Ohio National Guard and since 2008 has flown Medevac helicopters for Air Methods Corporation in Ohio.

Lorna McLearie

When World Airways was about to close its Oakland, California base in the late eighties Lorna was asked to manage a small interior design studio in Napa Valley. She was ready to leave San Francisco and live in a country, peaceful setting. World had given her the opportunity to do mostly international travel and gain exposure, which later assisted in design. She later worked as creative director and buyer for other showrooms while continuing her interior design and since 1999 has done so under her own name living in the more rural side of Napa.

A quote she loves is "The heart is the most exotic place in the world."

Joan Policastro

Joan is active in World Wings International, a philanthropic organization of former Pan Am flight attendants.

Queen Sirikit of Thailand
Official name: Somdet Phra Nang Chao Sirikit Phra Borommarachininat

Courtesy: www.kremlin.ru

The Queen mother of Thailand was 86 years old in 2019. She suffered a stroke in 2012 and has since refrained from public appearances.

Her birthday on August 12 is celebrated as a national holiday and Mother's Day in Thailand.

JoAnn Wright (Wintenburg) and Ken "Kip" Wintenburg

JoAnn and Kip

JoAnn enjoys herself searching for the gravestones of her ancestors all over America. She is cleaning tombstones as a volunteer at the Downey Cemetery in Downey, California. She is a member of the Daughters of the American Revolution and has several ancestors who fought in the Revolutionary and Civil Wars.

Kip Wittenberg continued with Continental Airlines and was an instructor on the DC-10 at age 33.

Kip Wittenberg 1978

After retiring from Continental, Kip flew seven years on a Boeing 777 for a Saudi Prince and now at 74 is a flight instructor on a TBM.

SOCATA TBM 900

Bea Weber

Bea, a flight Attendant for 45 years with Continental Airlines lives in Scottsdale, Arizona. She is in regular contact with other flight attendants and groups.

Bea Weber
Bea Weber at Continental reunion 2017

Bob Hirsch

Bob, a former Army Spec4 Vietnam veteran is retired and lives in San Diego, California with his wife Susan, a cancer survivor and artist/business owner.

Susan and Bob

Jim Sellers

Jim, a former Army Spec4 Vietnam veteran, is retired and lives in Mountain Lake, Minnesota with his wife Sherri.

After the war he graduated from Eastern Washington University and became a school teacher. Called to the ministry, he went to Fuller Theological Seminary and then pastored churches in Escondido, California and Portland, Oregon including his final church that had a Chinese congregation. Reflecting on those years Jim says, "What a privilege to serve in a cross-cultural setting to folks who were making the difficult transition to a new country and a new life. I learned much from their courage and faith."

Gretchen Bergstresser (Garren)

The former Airlift International flight attendant was married to an Air Force C-130 pilot based in Japan who flew into Viet Nam. Divorced and now remarried, she and her husband, Troy Avera own and operate a Bed & Breakfast (Avera-Clarke House) in Monticello, Florida. She also recently opened a vintage clothing store with a friend who has a Victorian tearoom.

Troy was an F-4 and F-14 Naval fighter pilot and retired as a Commander. He went on to fly for United Airlines and at age 65 flew for Panama flag carrier Copa Airlines.

Gretchen and Troy   Avera-Clarke Bed & Breakfast

Chapter 17
Reflections

This book is about the personal remembrances of special women and men who served America in an unusual way. Most of the memories are from women flight attendants and nearly all tell the stories of what happened in the past and how their experiences had a bearing on what the future would hold and shaped who they are today.

One of the ladies in the book who knows that to be true is my wife, Patti Medaris (Culea). She is a Godly woman who lives out her Christian faith daily. To me, the most important part of our marriage is a shared love for Jesus Christ and dependence on the Holy Spirit to direct our lives. Before we were married and in our 20's, we wandered far from our faith but God did not give up on us. We look back and can clearly see our Lord's Hand during our rebellious years and how He eventually brought us together to serve Him.

"My dream was to be a pilot," Patti says, "but in the late 50's and early 60's women were not encouraged to go into engineering, which was required for flight training. Looking back it is clear that God had another plan for my life that was far better than mine. God put me in a position to encourage young men as they prepared for a future they weren't sure of.

"I remember one young very scared Marine who noticed the cross necklace I wore. He was a believer and we prayed together for his safety while in Vietnam. I am sorry I never heard from him, nor do I remember his name.

"There were so many who professed their faith in Jesus. One I remember clearly, Captain Andy Ivan, who I met toward the end of his first tour in Vietnam.

Major Andrew Ivan, Jr.

"He was from Davis-Montham AFB in Tucson and was introduced to me by another officer I had met at Yokota AFB in Japan. Andy loved our Lord and we promised to keep in touch. Tragically, during his second combat tour he was shot down over Laos in September 1971. The Laotians were brutal and did not return our warriors. He was missing in action. At the time I heard his family opted not to have his name on the Vietnam wall, nor have a MIA bracelet made for him. Recently, I learned he was declared missing in action until August 23, 1978, when the Department of the Air Force changed his status to killed in action. His remains were located on August 31, 1994, and identified on March 7, 1996. I remembered Andy as a gentle, wonderful soul."

Author's notes:

Andrew Ivan Jr. was two weeks away from his 27th birthday when his F-4D Phantom fighter-bomber was shot down over the Plaine des Jarres in Laos on September 10, 1971.

F-4D Phantom over Vietnam

Also with Ivan was his backseat navigator Captain Leroy Cornwell III.

Captain Leroy J. Cornwell III

When the Phantom and the two men aboard failed to return to Udorn, an intensive air search was launched. A crash site was located near the village of Ban Ban in Xianghoang Province, Laos and air photos showed what appeared to be the main carriage of an F4 aircraft. No sign of Ivan or Cornwell was found.

Andrew Ivan, Jr. was from New Jersey and in the New Jersey Vietnam Veterans' Memorial website, friend John
Shelton wrote this:
"Andy was flying for the 13th TFS (Tactical Fighter Squadron) at Udorn

Air Base in Thailand in 1971 when he did not return home from a mission. He was flying as a High Speed Forward Air Controller at this time. Much of their work was in support of a secret war in northern Laos. This was a dangerous, all-volunteer unit that exposed themselves to heavy ground fire to find targets and report enemy movements. The crews would fly low to the ground (500 feet) at about 600 mph pulling high-G's at all times below the hilltops in bad weather. It took skill, experience and luck.

"Andy and I were roommates at flight school. He was not loud but very funny and well liked and often quoted. Men liked him and women chased him. He had no bad habits. He was neat, clean and respectful of others. He was not a choirboy. He was a man and a good one."

Andrew Ivan, Jr. and his navigator Leroy J. Cornwell, III are listed on the Vietnam Memorial Wall on Panel 2W, Line 13.

LEROY J CORNWELL III ANDREW IVAN Jr

While Ivan was an Air Force Captain when he was shot down, the Wall shows him as a Major. He and Cornwell are buried at Arlington National Cemetery with the date on their headstone September 28, 1973 the day they were declared dead.

Patti Medaris (Culea) says, "Reliving those times are often painful. I didn't talk about them much back then as most of my friends had no idea what was going on nor did they care. While I was living in Japan we would give the military overseas operators lots of goodies and they would connect us to our families Stateside. I had many tearful conversations with Grandma LeFever (Patti's mother's mother) in Illinois."

Patti (lower left) with her Grandmother LeFever
and sister Betty and cousins Michael and Annetta in the 1960's

Patti offered her thoughts to the author (her husband) in hopes of explaining why people of that era did what they did.

"I think an important part of the book," she says, "should be how we and the military let off steam and stress. Yes, there was a lot of drinking, gambling and partying, but there were also times when we'd get together and just talk, pray and read the Bible. I knew of Bible study groups in several places but because of my schedule, I wasn't able to get involved with any. However, I know they were a key part in helping many cope with what they were going through.

"The years 1969 and 1970 were truly a growing period in my life. I had come out of a really difficult time in my life and went back to being a flight attendant with Airlift.
I wasn't walking close to our Lord, but I know He was making me more aware of Him and that He had not forgotten me."

* * * * *

The flight home for Jim Sellers who spent one year in Vietnam from 1967-1968 was mentioned in an earlier chapter. Additional thoughts open the window to Jim's soul and that of other combat veterans who began their round-trip home.

Jim Sellers 1968   2019

"My own anxiety," Sellers remembers, "increased as we started down the runway. The only thing between me and arriving safely home was the completion of this long flight. At that moment I seemed to place all the dread and paranoia on that Flying Tiger flight. I had never been afraid to fly until that day and that fear stayed with me for many years.

"For this reason, the flight home was not a happy one. Every noise and each moment of turbulence filled me with a deeper sense of impending doom. I blame this reaction on my experiences in the war. Psychologist's call this 'transference.' I subconsciously placed my fear and dread on that flight. Vietnam was behind me, but my dread followed me home. Like most war veterans it took me many years to make peace with my experiences in harm's way."

Those experiences began in 1967 when he dropped an algebra class at Wenatchee Valley College in Washington state and was immediately classified 1A for the draft. To avoid a guaranteed infantry assignment, he enlisted in the Army for three years because the other service branches required a four-year stint.

He was trained in communications and cryptography and sent to an Army base west of Saigon near Long Binh, Vietnam; however, there was no need to decode the language and moral degeneracy that surrounded him.

Long Binh, South Vietnam

And, living through the Tet offensive where he saw wounded soldiers dying before they could be cared for left an indelible impression.

"These experiences brought my firm belief in God's providential care into conflict with the apparent randomness of war," says Jim. "It is difficult to explain what goes through your mind when you have no control of where the incoming rocket or mortar will land or which high-powered bullet will instantly end your life or the life of your comrade in arms. I never lost my deep faith in God but I had big questions for which I had no simple answers."

During his year in Vietnam, Jim promised himself if he survived, he would give his remaining life to something positive. He decided to return to college and marry his college girlfriend who had faithfully written to him during his time "in country."

The ugliness that surrounded him during war changed when it was time to go home. Greeting him at the airport in Bien Hoa near Saigon were pretty smiling faces of flight attendants.

"I flew home on Flying Tiger Airlines. It was clear to me then that this was not a glamorous assignment (for flight attendants). It was dangerous, very uncomfortable and they had to deal with a plane full of lonely soldiers that sometimes acted inappropriately. I think they deserve credit for their service to us and to the country. In spite of my fears, Flying Tiger Line and their pilots and stewardesses brought me safely home to what soldiers called 'the real world.'"

When Jim Sellers stepped off the plane at Travis Air Force base he kissed the tarmac.

* * * * *

Sometimes the events of that time were so brutally shocking they defied the ability to make sense of what happened, and, in some cases, recollections are still jumbled four decades later.

Lorna McLearie, a former World Airways flight attendant worked the last civilian flight out of Saigon on April 5, 1975. The day before she left, an Air Force C-5A cargo plane with 314 people on board, including many orphans crashed at Saigon's Tan Son Nhat Airport. The plane was airborne for 12 minutes before an explosion tore apart the lower rear fuselage. The crew could not get the plane back to the airport and it crashed in a rice paddy before hitting a dike and breaking into four parts. Seventy-eight children and 80 adults were killed.

Lorna says, "A friend of my mother's called her and asked if I was OK. My mother was shocked not hearing about it. She immediately called World scheduling in Oakland and they said, 'We have an emergency we can't talk now.'

"My mother said she felt ill, but later World scheduling returned her call to confirm I was safely in the Philippines. She had always been relieved she had three daughters first and my brothers in her late thirties because that spared the fear of losing a child to the Vietnam War.

"When I was caring for my mother the last few years of her life, we shared so many stories and it was then I learned that I never knew how much she worried about me.

"I realized later that I had kept some distance with the military because getting to know them would bring pain, knowing they might not return. I kept a professional distance and later was sorry I might have seemed too removed.

"Know that all of us cared deeply about the welfare of our passengers. I lost friends in Vietnam so my professional distance saved me emotionally."

* * * * *

After the war ended, there were still connections for Lorna with the people of Southeast Asia.

"In 1981," Lorna remembers, "I was based in Hong Kong to work refugee flights. The Vietnamese and Laotians had been in camps across Asia.

"They had endured so much, but had a quiet dignity about them. They were weary and tired, but their spirits were positive and hopeful. 'Fragile peace' always came to mind. Years later they have changed the face of many communities across America, making a positive difference."

* * * * *

It is impossible to comprehend the full impact and magnitude of the tragedy that touched hundreds of thousands of families who had loved ones and friends killed or wounded during the Vietnam War. A glimpse of that can be seen with Bob Hirsch of San Diego.

Bob served 16 months in combat with the 101st Airborne, 2nd Battalion, 506th Infantry Regiment and was one of many who came home profoundly changed by what he did and what he saw.

Perhaps the most traumatic moment was seeing what happened to his Army comrade, Specialist 4 (E-4) Darrell Clodfelter, a 20-year-old friend whose father, Donald, a B-24 pilot during World War II had been one of Bob's high school math teachers at Arlington High School in Indianapolis.

Darrell Clodfelter

"Darrell was a radio operator in charge of radio repairs and maintenance at our base camp," Bob says. "He hitched a ride on the mail-run helicopter out to one of the fire bases that were connected to our base camp named Camp Evans."

"He was going home soon and he wanted to say goodbye to his friends that were at that particular firebase. During the flight, an explosive devise took down the helicopter."

The crash was on January 12, 1971 at Thua Thien and Bob says what made it even more difficult was that he saw his friend's body when it was brought back to camp.

For 40 years, Bob Hirsch tried to deal on his own with Post Traumatic Stress Disorder (PTSD) until he reached out to the Veterans Administration in San Diego for help.

Two photos of Bob, side-by-side show the stark change that nearly every person who served on the front lines in Vietnam experienced. The first shows Bob as a new replacement for his unit and the second reflects what he went through.

Bob Hirsch newly arrived   Bob Hirsch later

Unlike some Veterans Administration (VA) facilities that are everything that is wrong with the system, Bob only has praise for the VA people in San Diego.

"When I first tried to get into the VA Healthcare System," Bob remembers, "my paperwork sat idle for almost six months. Every time I checked to see what my status was, I was assured that my paperwork was moving along.

"Eventually a friend suggested that I reach out for help from one of the volunteers at the VA hospital that are available to help with such matters. In my case, I ended up working with a volunteer from the Veterans of Foreign Wars (VFW). She was a 'God-send'. The day I walked into her office, she took my paperwork to the appropriate office at the VA and literally got the result I was waiting for that week!

"Once in the system, I started working with a therapist via both groups and one-on-one. It was a difficult series of PTSD-focused therapies that laid me bare to my very soul. It was a process that lasted two years, but I eventually got through it and today I have a better understanding of what I have been through, how it has affected me and that my fears and anger are now seen in a perspective that I can manage. My life is much richer now, I am more grateful for what I have, rather than what I may have lost. And I see how important the good folks I have gotten to know enrich the life I now have.

"It's all very hard to put into precise words, but for the first time in a very long time, I understand what it is to be truly grateful and humble instead of feeling angry and isolated. Love, friendship and the VA helped me get my life back."

* * * * *

In January 1975, President Gerald Ford stopped all U.S. military involvement in Vietnam. On April 30, 1975 communist forces over ran and seized Saigon bringing a quick surrender by the South Vietnam government.

Duong Van Minh, the last president of Vietnam escorted away by People's Army of Vietnam soldiers.

Other than those who were killed instantly, the government surrender was the only thing that happened quickly during the Vietnam War. The years dragged by and when it was over, millions of civilians and military troops had died or were wounded, and billions of dollars had been spent, all with a promise.

"I give you my pledge, we shall never let you down . . .

One day when they know peace, the whole world will acknowledge that what you have done here was worth the price."

President Lyndon B. Johnson
Addressing the troops in Cam Ranh Bay, South Vietnam
October 26, 1966

Chapter 18
In Memoriam

Edward Daly (1922-1984)

In 1975 the flamboyant World Airways owner fought Vietnamese soldiers who forced their way on board a 727 jetliner while he tried to get women and children on "The Last Flight Out of Da Nang." He then ordered and supervised the evacuation of orphans from Saigon. Daly retreated from business due to failing health in 1982 and two years later passed away at age 61.

Ken Healy (1916-2016)

Healy was the pilot on Ed Daly's orphan flights. The World War II Army Air Corps veteran was Vice President of Flight Operations at World Airways until his retirement in 1983. He celebrated his 100th birthday in 2016 and passed away two weeks later.

Charles Patterson (1925-1994)

Charles Patterson was a key figure in evacuating orphans and babies out of Vietnam. The World War II veteran was awarded the Silver Star, Bronze Star Medal and Purple Heart. He served as deputy director of the Peace Corps for Africa. Patterson joined World Airways in 1968 and retired as vice president and assistant to the president in 1985. He passed away at age 69.

Bruce Dunning (1940-2013)

The long time CBS News correspondent was on the World Airways famed "Last Flight Out Of Da Nang" in 1975. He died from injuries suffered in a fall at age 73.

Robert Macauley (1923-2010)

Philanthropist and businessman Robert Macauley came to the aid of 300 Vietnamese orphans stranded after a plane crash in Saigon. He chartered a Boeing 747 from Pan American World Airways to have the children leave the country, paying for the trip by mortgaging his house.

He passed away due to emphysema at age 87.

Creighton Abrams (1914-1974)

Abrams was a U.S. Army general who commanded military operations in the Vietnam War from 1968 to 1972. A heavy cigar smoker, Abrams died at age 59 from complications of surgery to remove a cancerous lung.

John Bruce Medaris (1902-1990)

Medaris was a retired Major General in the U.S. Army and later was part of America's space program. After recovering from bone cancer when he was 63 in 1965, the cancer returned and he passed away at age 88.

Bob Hope (1903-2003)

The legendary entertainer and movie star entertained troops for more than 50 years. He died of pneumonia at his home in Toluca Lake, California in 2003 reminding his fans of one of his classic lines just before his 100th birthday, "I'm so old, they've canceled my blood type."

Don Ho (1930-2007)

The singer and entertainer, best known for the song "Tiny Bubbles," passed away from a heart attack in his Waikiki apartment at age 76.

Robert Prescott (1913-1978)

The World War II ace with the American Volunteer Group better known as the Flying Tigers to fight the Japanese in China went on to found the Flying Tiger Line, the first scheduled cargo airline in the United States.

Prescott died of cancer at his Palm Springs, California home at age 64.

Dick Rossi (1915-2008)

Along with Robert Prescott, Rossi was a member of the American Volunteer Group (Flying Tigers) and was credited with 6 ¼ kills while fighting the Japanese in China. Rossi was among those who founded Flying Tiger Line and flew with the airline for 25 years. He passed away in 2008 at the age of 92 at his home in Fallbrook, California from complications of pneumonia.

Lloyd "Pete" Bucher (1927-2004)

Bucher was the commanding officer of USS Pueblo that was seized by North Korea in 1968. He and his crew were held as prisoners for 11 months.

Bucher, given up for adoption by his birth mother lived in a series of orphanages until he was accepted at the famous Father Flanagan's Boy's Town. He dropped out his senior year to enlist in the Navy during World War II and reached the rank of quartermaster second class before entering the University of Nebraska on a football scholarship. While in college he signed up for Naval ROTC and graduated in 1953 with a BS degree and was commissioned an Ensign in the Naval Reserve.

Called to active duty the following year, Bucher served aboard submarines before being given command of Pueblo.

By most accounts, the U.S. government failed to support Bucher when the ship was captured and although a recommended court martial never happened and Bucher was not found guilty of any indiscretions, his Navy career was tarnished and he retired in the rank of commander.

The author got to know Bucher and his wife Rose and would have been honored to serve under him.

Pete Bucher passed away in Poway, California. He was 76.

Bhumibol Adulyadej King of Thailand

2006

The King reigned as an adult for 70 years and 126 days, the longest-reigning monarch in Thai history. He passed away in 2016 at age 88.

John David "Eric" Erickson (1943-2005)

"Eric" Erickson who met Patti Medaris (Culea) and dated her for several months left the Air Force and was hired by a CIA support airline called Continental Air Service.

He returned stateside and found a home with Flying Tiger Line that later was bought by Federal Express. Eric ended his professional flying career as a FedEx Captain.

Eric and his wife, Frieda spent many years living in Alaska where he flew his own Cessna 185 and helped support flying missions for the Iditarod. He passed away in 2015 at age 71.

Chapter 19
Remembering the Airlines

Air America

Air America was an American passenger and cargo airline covertly owned and operated by the US government. It originally was Civil Air Transport (CAT) a Nationalist Chinese airline founded in 1946 that was reorganized as Air America in 1959.

Air America was used as a dummy corporation for Central Intelligence Agency (CIA) operations in Indochina and ceased operations in 1976.

Air Vietnam

Air Vietnam, founded in 1951, was South Vietnam's first commercial air carrier. Flight crews were composed of civilian, ex-military pilots (mostly former Republic of Vietnam Air Force), along with a few Americans. The airline was active during the Vietnam War and flew more than a million passengers before ceasing operations when Saigon collapsed on April 30, 1975.

Airlift International

Airlift International was founded by John Riddle and operated by the American Central Intelligence Agency from 1945 and ceased operations in 1991. It was headquartered at Miami International Airport in unincorporated Miami-Dade County, Florida.

Capitol Air

Capitol Air was a charter airline that was founded in 1946. It filed for bankruptcy in 1984 after its owner, George Batchelor had largely dismantled the airline in favor of newly acquired Arrow Air that became a scheduled passenger airline. Arrow Air went bankrupt in 1986 following a DC-8 jetliner crash in Newfoundland, killing 248 American soldiers.

Flying Tiger Line

Flying Tiger Line, also known as Flying Tigers, was the first scheduled cargo airline in the United States and a major military charter operator during the Cold War era for both cargo and personnel. It was founded in 1945 and was bought by Federal Express in 1988.

Northwest Orient Airlines

Northwest Airlines Corp. was a major United States airline founded in 1926 and after increased competition from low-cost airlines and labor problems it was absorbed into Delta Air Lines, Inc. by a merger in 2008. The merger made Delta the largest airline in the world until the American Airlines-US Airways merger on December 9, 2013.

Note: In 1967 the author was transferred from Commander Naval Forces, Korea in Seoul to the Naval Communications Unit in London, England and flew Northwest Airlines to the United States before continuing to England. A line heard often in Korea for returning military personnel was "catching the red tail home."

A perspective on Northwest Airlines comes from Terry Johnson, a retired pilot who flew for Republic Airlines when it was bought by Northwest. Writing in the book *The Friday Pilots*, edited by Don Shepperd, AuthorHouse 2014, Johnson said "Overnight, I and everyone else at Republic went from one of the best workplaces to one of the worst. Republic was a great, small airline with a wonderful working environment. Northwest was plagued with labor disputes and unhappy employees. Northwest slowly improved with the involvement of outside investors and changes in management. Today as part of Delta, it is one of the best places to work."

Overseas National Airways

The original Overseas National Airways Inc. was an American airline, formed in June 1950 and ceased operations in 1986.

Pan American World Airways

Pan American World Airways was the principal and largest international air carrier and unofficial flag carrier of the United States from 1927 until its financial collapse on December 4, 1991.

A perspective on the airline's demise comes from Joan Policastro, a long-time flight attendant. She thinks there were two main reasons the end came for Pan Am. The first was Pan Am's decision to purchase National Airlines in 1980 for more than $400 million.

The second reason that sealed Pan Am's doom was the bombing and crash of Pan Flight 103 over Scotland in 1988 that killed 259 on the Boeing 747 and eleven people on the ground.

Photo Courtesy: AAIB, UK 1990

Saturn Airways

Saturn Airways was a U.S. charter airline. It operated from 1948 until it ceased operations in 1976.

In 1972, Saturn took over the assets of defunct Universal Airlines before being absorbed by Trans International Airlines in 1976.

Seaboard World Airlines

Seaboard World Airlines was an international all-cargo airline founded in 1946 and based in the United States. The airline merged with Flying Tiger Line in 1980 and is now part of FedEx Airlines.

Southern Air Transport

Southern Air Transport, founded in 1947 and based in Miami, Florida, was a cargo airline best known as a front company for the Central Intelligence Agency. It ceased operations in 1998.

Trans International Airlines

Trans International Airlines was an airline that offered charter service from and within the United States. It also operated scheduled passenger service flying as Transamerica Airlines as well as charter flights during its last decade. Founded in 1947 by Kirk Kerkorian, TIA ceased operations in 1986.

Universal Airlines

Universal Airlines was a United States airline that operated from 1966 to 1972 (see above).

World Airways

World Airways, Inc. was an American airline headquartered operating non-scheduled services. World Airways ceased all operations in April 2014.

However, nine years earlier in 2005 there was a dramatic moment of glory for the gutsy airline. On June 13 of that year, in a flight filled with drama, memories and tears, a shiny World Airways MD-11 freshly re-painted in the same red and white company colors worn by the fleet in 1975 prepared to take off from Oakland. It would be bound for Vietnam and the passengers on board included 21 of the former orphans World had rescued from Saigon in a series of flights known as "Operation Babylift."

Operation Babylift adoptees pose with former World Airways executives
and other distinguished guests
Photo: Courtesy Airport Journals

Before departing there was a news conference at KaiserAir across from
Hanger 5, which was World Airways original hanger when the company
began operations in Oakland in the 1950's.

Photo: Courtesy Airport Journals

Randy Martinez, the CEO of World Air Holdings stated, "We're here to
honor our heritage and recognize the contribution of our employees."

The passenger manifest for World Airways Flight #001 contained 112
names, several right out of 30-year-old newspaper headlines. Included were

pilots, flight attendants and other World personnel that had risked their lives to save orphan children and refugees along with decorated Vietnam veterans and distinguished members of World's board of directors, management team and their guests.

Pilots Bill Keating (90 in 2005) and Ken Healy (89 in 2005) flew the original Operation Babylift flight from Saigon on April 2, 1975
Photo: Courtesy Airport Journals

One of those on that flight was Jan Wollett.

"I wasn't sure how I would feel going back," she said. "We flew over Da Nang, then into Saigon," Wollett said. "As we taxied up, people applauded. You knew the war is over for them. I wish the healing could have come here as quickly."

And while not listed on the manifest, there was no doubt the spirit of World Airways maverick president and owner Ed Daly was on board the flight.

Ed Daly

* * * * *

A darker side of the airlines involves many flight attendants who missed out in retirement benefits.

"I flew for 17 years," says former World Airways flight attendant Lorna McLearie, "and left with a severance check of $2,700. Retirement started when I left in 1987 but I have no regrets in leaving, as I have had an interesting career in design."

Norma McLearie (center) 1981

Chapter 20
Recognition

Thousands of women, who accompanied troops to and from Vietnam as flight attendants, served our nation in a remarkable way. Not all of them embraced the "why'" of the Vietnam War, but every one of them held the soldiers, Marines, sailors and airmen who were on their planes close to their hearts.

With that said, should formal recognition be given for what they did?

In Washington, D.C. there is a memorial dedicated to thousands of women of the United States who served during the Vietnam War.

First enlisted women in the Air Force assigned to Vietnam arrive in country 1967

As many as 10,000 of them were nurses and that is represented in a sculpture at the Vietnam Women's Memorial located on National Mall a short distance south of The Wall and north of the Reflecting Pool.

Vietnam Women's Memorial

The Vietnam Women's Memorial was established to honor those women who served and also the families who lost loved ones in the war, so they would know about the women who provided comfort, care, and a human touch for those who were suffering and dying.

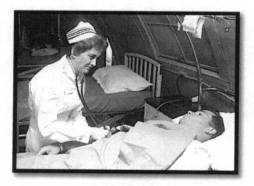

U.S. Navy nurse LCDR Joan Brouilette
1968

While combat nurses were the ones most often at the hospital bedsides of wounded troops, there were many flight attendants who went out of their way to visit soldiers, Marines, airmen and sailors in hospitals.

One in particular was Gretchen Bergstresser (Garren).

"While living in Japan with Airlift, one of my roommates was dating a Marine liaison officer stationed there. He invited us to the hospital that I think was located at Camp Zama. These were the soldiers that were too severely injured and didn't think they would survive the trip back stateside. This was considered our goodwill tour, he told us to make ourselves beautiful and wear the shortest skirt we had. He reminded us that these guys were all alone and seriously injured and needed their morale boosted. No matter what, no tears and be fun and positive. As I recall whoever was home went with him to the hospital on Sundays. We sang, talked, laughed, and wrote letters home for them. What stands out the most about these trips was how proud these guys were to be a Marine. It was truly amazing.

* * * * * *

Another touching memory comes from Continental Airlines flight attendant Bea Weber.

Bea Weber

Bea's visits were to the hospital at Clark Air Force Base in the Philippines where many wounded troops were evacuated. She noticed that patients who had their legs in a cast would have an opening for their toes to stick out.

"Since my father was a doctor, I knew that their toes would get cold," she remembers, "so I began knitting toe-warmers that slipped over the casts. Others joined me and the project caught on. We would put messages on the toe-warmers with words like 'Thank You,' or "Come Home Soon.' It wasn't long before ladies at a Presbyterian Church in Beverly Hills took on the project and we were sending toe-warmers by the box full."

* * * * *

Other flight attendants also used layover time to visit troops recovering in hospitals in Okinawa and Tachikawa. And if not at hospitals, each smiling face provided more than their share of comfort, care and a human touch within the confines of jetliners, on airport tarmacs and at military bases from the United States all across the Pacific and in Vietnam.

Jeannie Wagers (Wiseman)
1960's

Their personal devotion brought a priceless connection to young men who were about to enter hell on earth or for those who had escaped the same.

Courtesy: JPB Transconsulting

The official stated mission of the Vietnam Women's Memorial Project is to promote the healing of thousands of Vietnam women veterans through the placement of a memorial on the grounds of the Vietnam Veterans Memorial in Washington, D.C.; to identify the military and civilian women who served during the Vietnam war; to educate the public about their role; and to facilitate research on the physiological, psychological, and sociological issues correlated to their service.

Former World Airways flight attendant Helen Tennant (Hegelheimer) was at the Vietnam Women's Memorial dedication in 1993 and says civilian women that were in Vietnam were honored as well as the military women.

Helen Tennant (Hegelheimer)

"The founders of the memorial," she says, "are very much aware that more civilian women were in Vietnam during that long war then military women. I personally, do not see the Women's memorial as a salute to just nurses.

"If you research the difficulty that the founders had to get the Women's memorial built on the Mall, then I think you'll understand why it had to be as military oriented as it is. But at no time during the dedication or since, have civilian women ever been 'excluded' from the memorial, quite the contrary."

Former World Airways flight attendant Lorna McLearie brings up a valid point about how to recognize women who served on Military Airlift Command (MAC) flights.

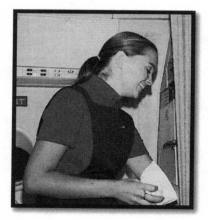

Lorna McLearie in DC-8 galley
1970

"I do not know how there could be enough data to track the thousands of flight attendants to give proper credit," she says. "I think most carry a personal pride in knowing they were there and did their best. Personally, I struggled with not being sensitive enough.

"However, I do believe most flight attendants never expected recognition for their trips into Vietnam. It was just part of our job and most of the military were young like we were. On one flight I was working the aft galley and a guy stopped me and knew my name. He had been my biology partner in high school. He seemed to have grown a foot and was so sweet. I was relieved I was working his trip out. I think his name was Rick."

* * * * *

In isolated cases, some airlines included hazardous duty pay for flight attendants and there were military units that recognized the service of flight attendants.

Former World Airways flight attendant Janet Bancroft (Burttram) said, "The military gave flight attendants a certificate once they completed 100 take offs and landings in Vietnam. They acknowledged our being in the war zone and I wish I still had it."

Janet Bancroft (Burttram) (top right)

* * * * *

Helen Tennant (Hegelheimer) commenting on that writes, "I didn't know there was a certificate for 100 landings in country . . . must have happened after my time (1966-1967) at World Airways. How cool!"

* * * * *

On The Wall in Washington, D.C. are more than 58,000 names, including eight women who lost their lives in combat.

While the author could not find any record of a flight attendant who was killed or seriously wounded while working Military Airlift Command flights, there is no denying they endured psychological trauma with grace and poured out immeasurable comfort.

Former Flying Tiger Line and Airlift International flight attendant Patti Medaris (Culea) says, "I think we thought we were just another group of people on the sidelines doing our job. While living in Japan I remember my roommate Vicki said we should get some kind of recognition, but we all felt that it was just our job as flight attendants.

"I'm not sure who to go to for this type of thing (getting recognition). But, in listening to the men who flew on those flights, they were the important ones and we cared. We tried to bring joy to these terribly young men who were going into harm's way, and for what? But, that is another story."

* * * * *

Typical of many women who served selflessly is Helen Tennant (Hegelheimer). "Three million military men went to Vietnam during the war," she says. "No one gave a damn about them. I consider it an honor to have helped some of them make that 24-hour transition from war to home. I just don't need badges."

And she adds, "I don't need any recognition from any official regarding what I did during the Vietnam War. Running into a Vietnam Vet and telling him I was a 'Freedombird' and watching his face light up is better than anything 'official'. And BTW, let's not forget that there were stewardesses/flight attendants that carried troops during the first Gulf War and the Iraqi and Afghan wars. They're just like we were!"

* * * * *

Fredene Weaver (Maulhardt) who flew with World Airways for five years says she and her fellow flight attendants were only interested in doing their best from the sidelines and didn't expect special recognition then and not now.

Fredene (Weaver) Maulhardt then and now

What she came away with was the knowledge that she and her colleagues did something very special that mattered greatly and helped countless young men make it through the most difficult time of their lives.

* * * * *

In 2023, it will have been 50 years since the Vietnam War officially ended and 30 years since the Women's Vietnam Memorial was dedicated. It is likely that a ceremony will be held in 2023 at all of the memorials. There could be a Congressional proclamation prepared recognizing the contribution of women flight attendants during one of our nation's most difficult eras. But then again, it is obvious those women who served don't need a reminder of what they did.

Chapter 21
Acknowledgements

Without the help of many people and organizations, this book would not have been possible. The idea came from my wife, Patti who as you have read was in the middle of the Vietnam War as a flight attendant for Flying Tiger Line and Airlift International. Gleaning her many stories added to my admiration for her. She is a remarkable woman and as a cancer survivor since 2013, is the most courageous person I have ever known.

* * * * *

Former Flying Tiger Line pilot George Gewehr was also an invaluable resource for the book. As the historian for the Flying Tiger Line Pilots Association his knowledge of aircraft and all of what pilots and crewmembers went through provided extraordinary insight that brought the story alive.
* * * * *

Janet Bancroft (Burttram) was a constant contributor to the manuscript and providing vivid memories while connecting me with former colleagues to keep the project moving forward.
* * * * *

Lorna McLearie made major contributions to the book recalling her years with World Airways.
* * * * *

JoAnn Wright (Wintenburg) and Ken Wintenburg provided many photos and memories that gave special insight. JoAnn also put me in touch with former colleague Bea Weber who supplied wonderful stories.

* * * * *

Jeannie Wagers (Wiseman) gave her unique insight on all things World Airways and was a constant source of colorful and memorable material.

* * * * *

Fredene Weaver (Maulhardt) helped the author keep things in perspective with sensitive observations and helpful advice.

* * * * *

BJ Elliott, a former Continental Airlines flight attendant provided wonderful insight and photos through her book *Behind My Wings*. During correspondence about her memories, she put me in touch with former colleagues. She is a dynamic, devout Christian who is available to speak at churches and veterans groups.
                              * * * * *

Joan Policastro enthusiastically shared her memories that gave new understanding of what flight attendants faced then and what they carry in their hearts today.

Grateful thanks to many others include:

Air America: (Excerpt from *Warrior Culture of the U.S. Marines*, copyright 2001 Marion F. Sturkey)

Airport Journals, "Courage Revisited--World Airways Returns to Vietnam," August 1, 2005

John Dickson, President
Flying Tiger Pilots Association

Lydia Rossi
Bob Hirsch
Bea Weber
Jim Sellers
Marsha Hay (Merz)
Julie Murtough (Gewehr)
Flying Tigers Club
Flying Tigers Pilots Association
Wikipedia

MIV
Military Bases.Com
USMC Heritage Press
CIA
Francois Sully Photo Collection, Vietnam March 1965

"Which is Safer: Airplanes or Cars?" Aric Jenkins, *Fortune* magazine, July 20, 1917

Heroic World Airlines Pilots Flew Overloaded 727 on Last Flight Out Of Da Nang by Bill Walton

Cicina Norton, President, Retiree Association of Flight Attendants

Pan Am Historical Society
U.S. Air Force

"Chaos in the air" Steve Lathrop *Albany Democrat-Herald*
Jan 22, 2012

Flight Attendant Recalls Vietnam War R & R Service, John Ruch, Reporter Newspapers, November 9, 2018

Making a difference: Robert Macauley, The $12 billion man, *Bangor Daily News*, Dave Riley, April 29, 2015

The American Homefront Project, *Flight Attendant On Saigon Evacuation: You Wanted 'To Help Every Child'* Patricia Murphy, April 28, 2015

Sylvia Wrigley's Fear of Landing
The Mystery of Flying Tiger Line Flight 739
September 30, 2016

Steve Priske Pan Am Historical Society

Frank Coffey "Fifty Years with the USO," New York: Brassey's Inc. 1991

New Jersey Vietnam Veterans' Memorial
Captain Andrew Ivan photos and information

Next Avenue. The Vietnam War, PBS

Top 10 Vietnam Era Songs, Thirteen.org

20th-Century Fashion, Thames & Hudson, John Peacock, 1993

Index

A

McChord AFB 29, 48, 134, 210
Robert Macauley 77-78, 276, 306
Major General John Medaris 145, 278